STANDARD LEGAL FORMS AND AGREEMENTS FOR CANADIAN BUSINESS

Edited by
Stephen L.P. Sanderson, LL.B., LL.M.

Self-Counsel Press
(a division of)
International Self-Counsel Press Ltd.
Canada   USA

Printed in Canada.

First edition: 1989
Reprinted: 1990; 1991; 1992; 1993; 1994; 1996; 1998; 1999; 2000; 2002; 2004
Second edition: 2005
Reprinted: 2007

Library and Archives Canada Cataloguing in Publication

Standard legal forms and agreements for Canadian business / edited by Stephen L.P. Sanderson. — 2nd ed.

(Self-counsel legal series)
ISBN 1-55180-650-9

1. Business law—Canada—Forms. 2. Contracts—Canada—Forms.
I. Sanderson, Stephen L. P. II. Series.

HF5371.S73 2005	346.7107'0269	C2005-903342-8

Self-Counsel Press
(a division of)
International Self-Counsel Press Ltd.

1481 Charlotte Road	1704 North State Street
North Vancouver, BC V7J 1H1	Bellingham, WA 98225
Canada	USA

CONTENTS

NOTICE TO READERS   vi

INTRODUCTION   vii

1   DOCUMENT SET-UPS   1

Form 100 Full block letter style   2

Form 101 Semi-block letter style   3

Form 102 Memorandum set-up   4

Form 103 Formal corporate signature set-up   5

2   NEW BUSINESSES   6

Form 200 Proposal to buy a business   8

Form 201 Agreement of purchase and sale of business assets (with full warranties)   9

Form 202 Agreement of purchase and sale of business assets (with limited warranties)   14

Form 203 Agreement of purchase and sale of shares   18

Form 204 Partnership agreement   23

Form 205 Joint venture agreement   27

Form 206 Partnership agreement checklist   31

Form 207 Distribution agreement   34

Form 208 Commission sales agreement   38

Form 209 Business plan checklist   41

3   SERVICES   45

Form 300 Engagement of services   46

Form 301 Engagement of another's services   47

Form 302 Independent contractor agreement   48

Form 303 Authorized extras   50

Form 304 Change work order   51

4   EMPLOYMENT   52

Form 400 Rejecting employment application   54

Form 401 Confirming employment terms   55

Form 402 Employment agreement   57

Form 403 Employee warning notice   60

Form 404 Employee dismissal notice   61

Form 405 Employee covenants: secrecy/non-competition   62

Form 406 Employee covenant: expense recovery   63

Form 407 Employee invention covenant   64

5   BUYING   65

Form 500 Invitation to quote price of goods   67

Form 501 Demand for delivery of goods   68

Form 502 Cancellation of purchase order for late delivery   69

Form 503 Rejection of non-conforming goods   70

Form 504 Partial rejection of non-conforming goods   71

Form 505 Request for instruction to return rejected goods   72

Form 506 Conditional acceptance of non-conforming goods   73

Form 507 Election to return goods on approval   74

Form 508 Conditional payment for goods reserving rights   75

Form 509 Notice of defective goods   76

Form 510 Stop payment on cheque   77

6   SELLING   78

Form 600 Bill of sale   80

Form 601 Bill of sale (without warranties)   81

Form 602 Bill of sale (with encumbrances)   82

Form 603 Receipt for goods   83

Form 604 Demand for particulars of rejection of goods   84

Form 605 Refusal of rejection of goods   85

Form 606 Delivery of substituted goods   86

Form 607 Rejected goods return instructions   87

Form 608 Replacing rejected goods   88

Form 609 Inability to fill purchase order   89

Form 610 Late delivery of goods   90

Form 611 Liability exclusion clause   91

Form 612 Limited warranty   92

7   COLLECTIONS   93

Form 700 Request for payment   94

Form 701 Second request for payment   95

Form 702 Final demand for payment   96

Form 703 Bad cheque letter   97

Form 704 Installment payment agreement   98

Form 705 Receipt for payment   100

Form 706 Collection instructions to lawyers   101

Form 707 Notice of disputed account   102

Form 708 Settlement offer of disputed account   103

Form 709 Agreement to compromise disputed account   104

8   CREDIT/DEBIT   105

Form 800 Personal credit application   107

Form 801 Authority to release credit information   109

Form 802 Demand promissory note   110

Form 803 Joint and several demand promissory note   111

Form 804 Due date promissory note   112

Form 805 Series form promissory note   113

Form 806 Periodic payment promissory note   114

Form 807 Demand for payment on demand promissory note   115

Form 808 Payment in full demand on installment promissory note   116

Form 809 Installment payment demand on promissory note   117

Form 810 Guarantee   118

Form 811 Demand for payment on guarantee   119

9 LEASES 120

    Form 900 Commercial lease 121

    Form 901 Exercising option to renew lease 125

    Form 902 Notice of rent default 126

    Form 903 Notice of other lease default 127

    Form 904 Landlord notice of termination of lease 128

    Form 905 Tenant notice of termination of lease 129

    Form 906 Agreement to cancel lease 130

    Form 907 Assignment of lease 131

    Form 908 Amendment of lease 133

    Form 909 Commercial sublease 134

10 ASSIGNMENTS 136

    Form 1000 Assignment with warranties 137

    Form 1001 Assignment without warranties 138

    Form 1002 Assignment of money due 139

    Form 1003 Assignment of real estate contract 140

    Form 1004 Assignment of contract 141

    Form 1005 Assignment of copyright 142

    Form 1006 Notice of assignment 143

    Form 1007 Cheque endorsements 144

11 CORPORATE 145

    Form 1100 Notice of annual meeting of shareholders 147

    Form 1101 Notice of special meeting of shareholders 148

    Form 1102 Proxy form 149

    Form 1103 Notice of meeting of directors 150

    Form 1104 Minutes of shareholders' meeting 151

    Form 1105 Minutes of directors' meeting 152

    Form 1106 Shareholders' resolutions 153

    Form 1107 Directors' resolutions 154

    Form 1108 Bylaw 155

    Form 1109 Annual directors' resolutions 156

    Form 1110 Annual shareholders' resolutions 157

    Form 1111 Other directors' resolutions 158

    Form 1112 Other shareholders' resolutions 159

    Form 1113 Resignation of officer 160

    Form 1114 Resignation of director 161

    Form 1115 Certificate of true copy 162

12 MISCELLANEOUS 163

    Form 1200 Unilateral release of liability 164

    Form 1201 Mutual release of liability 165

    Form 1202 Trade secret non-disclosure agreement 166

    Form 1203 Declaration of trust 167

NOTICE TO READERS

INTRODUCTION

This book is a manual of standard business and legal forms designed to save you time and money drawing up letters and documents in your business and personal affairs.

Most of the forms and their accompanying notes were drafted by practising Canadian professionals and are based on common law principles applicable throughout most of North America.

Please note: The purpose of this compilation is to provide a ready source of written forms for use in standard, unambiguous situations. Laws vary from jurisdiction to jurisdiction and specific situations may involve disputed crucial facts or special legal considerations.

A lawyer should be consulted for legal advice in any case of doubt as to proper use of a form in a specific situation. It is your responsibility to determine whether you need legal advice in connection with the use of a form but, even when you decide to seek legal advice, the form will provide a time-saving basis for the consultation.

1. HOW TO USE THIS BOOK

There are 111 forms in this book, divided into 12 chapters: Document Set-ups, New Businesses, Services, Employment, Buying, Selling, Collections, Credit/Debit, Leases, Assignments, Corporate and Miscellaneous. The forms are numbered within each chapter. You can easily find the form you want by referring to the Contents at the front of the book.

Guidelines on the purpose and use of the forms are given at the beginning of each chapter. Further instructions are printed on the forms themselves where needed. The various letter templates in chapter 1 are filled in as samples to show the formatting. You can either type your own forms using these as samples, or use the letter templates provided on the CD-ROM. Most forms and contracts in the book are blank templates that can be photocopied and filled in.

On the CD-ROM all forms are provided in both MS Word and PDF formats for use on a Windows-based PC. If you wish to customize forms with your letterhead, or modify them to suit your particular circumstances, use the forms in MS Word.

2. NOTES ON FORMALITIES

2.1 Seals

Many of the forms are drafted to be given or executed "under seal." To "seal" a document, the common practice today is to place a small red sticker or wafer next to the signature of the people executing it. This is a holdover from the days when wax impressions were used to record a person's personal seal of promise. Red wafers, or seals, are available in most stationery stores. If you do not have a ready supply of little red seals, just have the person signing draw a little circle around the little "s" at the end of the signature line for the desired effect.

2.2 Corporate signatures

The normal contracts/covenants have been mainly drafted in contemplation of execution by individuals. If something has to be executed by or on behalf of a corporation, use the formal corporate signature set-up in Form 103.

It is possible to bind a corporation on the individual signature of someone authorized to sign on behalf of the corporation, but it should be clearly stated that the individual is signing on behalf of the corporation and not in his or her own personal capacity.

Using the formal corporate set-up makes this abundantly clear. Actually affixing the corporate seal to the signature line is desirable but not absolutely necessary.

3. WHEN YOU NEED OTHER FORMS

Self-Counsel Press publishes a variety of business and other forms packages. The *Small Business Forms* kit contains all the forms you need to a run a small business, including forms for accounting, meeting agendas, personnel, purchasing, reports, and sales. For these and other professional ready-to-use forms on CD-ROM, visit our website at <www.self-counsel.com>.

1
DOCUMENT SET-UPS

Form 100. Full block letter style

This sample illustrates the full block style of letter set-up.

Form 101. Semi-block letter style

This sample illustrates the semi-block style of letter set-up.

Form 102. Memorandum set-up

This sample illustrates a set-up for internal office memoranda.

Form 103. Formal corporate signature set-up

This sample illustrates how to set up a formal corporate signature line on a contract. No independent witness is required for a corporate seal signature even where the contract or document calls for one signature because the seal is the corporation's signature and the witness is the officer signing the impression of the seal. The "c/s" refers to and reminds you to impress the corporate seal of the company.

FULL BLOCK LETTER STYLE

January 1, 20--

Any Company Ltd.
12 Any Street
Anytown, Anyprovince
A1A 1Z1

Attention: John H. Doe, President

Dear Sir:

Re Full Block Letter Style

Further to your query, we use what is commonly known as a "full block" style of letter set-up for use with a printed letterhead.

As this letter demonstrates, each part of the letter begins flush with the left-hand margin.

The choice of letter set-up may be affected by the physical limitations of your printed letterhead. However, other things being equal, the "full block" style of letter set-up is the easiest to type.

In closing, please note that this letter is composed in the first person plural ("we") as though it comes from our business rather than from any particular individual. This means that the signature line should reflect the business as well.

Very truly yours,

Acme Letter Writing Inc.

per:

R.J. Roe, Customer Relations

copy to Customer Records
RR/ss

SEMI-BLOCK LETTER STYLE

Acme Letter Writing Inc.
1 Any Road
Anycity, Anyprovince
Z1Z 1A1

January 1, 20--

Jane L. Doe
12 Home Street
Anytown, Anyprovince
A1A 1Z1

Dear Ms. Doe:

Re Semi-Block Letter Style

Further to your query, I use what is commonly known as a "semi-block" style of letter set-up.

As you can see from this letter, the inside address and opening salutation begin flush with the left-hand margin.

However, the date and any return address (where you are not using a printed letterhead) are typed in the upper right-hand corner. Also, the first line of each paragraph is indented and the complimentary closing and any underlined subject line between the opening salutation and the first paragraph are usually centred.

I use the "semi-block" style of letter set-up because it most closely resembles the way I was taught to write a letter by hand.

In closing, please note that I have composed this letter in the first person singular ("I") as though it comes specifically from me rather than from my business. This means that the signature should emphasize me as well.

Very truly yours,

Richard J. Roe

RJR/ss

MEMORANDUM

To:

From:

Date:

Subject:

4

FORMAL CORPORATE SIGNATURE

_____
(full corporate name)

per:_____c/s
(signer's name, office)

as in

ACME LETTER WRITING INC.

per: _____c/s
Richard J. Roe, President

2
NEW BUSINESSES

Form 200. Proposal to buy a business

You may want to find out whether the owner of a business is prepared to sell it in principle before going to the time and trouble of making a formal, potentially legally binding, offer. Use this form to sound out a proposal to purchase a business. Fill in the forms with the pertinent information.

Form 201. Agreement of purchase and sale of business assets (with full warranties)

Use this form, with proper legal and accounting advice, to make a formal offer for the purchase and sale of the assets of a business. Note that the allocation of the total purchase price between the specific assets may have significant tax consequences for both parties. Note also the wide warranty protection in the agreement which is to the advantage of the purchaser.

In section 1.02, list exclusions (e.g., cash on hand or on deposit, accounts receivable, book and other debts due or accruing due).

Form 202. Agreement of purchase and sale of business assets (with limited warranties)

Use this form, with proper legal and accounting advice, to prepare a formal agreement of purchase and sale of business assets with limited warranty protection for the benefit of the purchaser. Note that the allocation of the total purchase price between the specific assets may have significant tax consequences for both parties. Note also the limitations of warranties as to quality and fitness for purpose and the non-survival of all warranties which is to the advantage of the vendor.

In section 1.02, list exclusions (e.g., cash on hand or on deposit, accounts receivable, book and other debts due or accruing due).

Form 203. Agreement of purchase and sale of shares

There are two ways to buy a business owned by a corporation: by buying the assets of the business and by buying the corporation itself. The disadvantages of buying the corporation is that you are acquiring a package of assets and liabilities. You can ask for warranties from the vendor about liabilities, but the simple fact of the matter is that it is impossible to independently check out all the potential liabilities. On the other hand, the purchase of a corporation may have certain income tax advantages. Use this form, with proper accounting and legal advice, to prepare a simple agreement for the purchase and sale of the shares of a corporation.

Form 204. Partnership agreement

Use this form, with proper legal advice, to prepare a simple partnership agreement between two or more partners. It is important to realize that partnership, like marriage, should not be entered into lightly. Partners have wide apparent authority to personally bind the other partners. Note, however, that a partnership agreement only governs the relationship between the partners, and limitations on a partner's actual authority will probably not affect dealings with third parties who have no knowledge of the terms of the partnership agreement. Nonetheless, there is great value in spelling out the relationship between the partners.

Form 205. Joint venture agreement

Use this form, with proper legal advice, to prepare a formal joint venture agreement between two or more partners. Note that a joint venture is, in law, a partnership for a particular venture.

(See guidelines for Form 204.)

Form 206. Partnership agreement checklist

Use the checklist on this form to map out a proposed partnership agreement.

Form 207. Distribution agreement

Use this form with proper legal advice, to draft a distribution agreement for the supply and re-sale of specific products.

Note that the form is set up for corporate signatures (with a personal guarantee provision for the individual behind the distributor corporation) but you can set it up for an individual distributor signature and delete the references to guarantee.

Form 208. Commission sales agreement

Use this form, with proper legal advice, to draft a commission sales agreement where an agent agrees to sell specific products on behalf of a principal for a commission.

Form 209. Business plan checklist

Prior to seeking any major financing for a business, it is a good idea to prepare a business plan. It should set out in detail what the business is about and how the principals expect to accomplish their short- and long-term goals. It often becomes part of the financing contract. Use this form to ensure that your business plan is complete.

PROPOSAL TO BUY A BUSINESS

_____, 20___

Attention:

Dear _____:

Re Purchase of _____
(name of business)

We are interested in negotiating an agreement for the purchase and sale as a going concern of all the business assets, including furniture, fixtures and equipment, stock in trade, parts and supplies, leasehold interest and goodwill, owned by you in connection with the_____
(type of business)

business carried on as_____
(name of business)

at _____
(address)

Subject to formal contract, we are prepared to pay $ _____for the business on the following terms:

If you are interested in selling at this price on these terms, please let us know and we will make you a formal offer to purchase.

Yours very truly,

_____
(Signature)

AGREEMENT OF PURCHASE AND SALE OF BUSINESS ASSETS
(WITH FULL WARRANTIES)

This agreement of purchase and sale is made in two original copies between

(1)_____
        (the "Vendor")

and

(2) _____
        (the "Purchaser")

SUBJECT MATTER

1.01 The Purchaser agrees to buy and the Vendor agrees to sell to the Purchaser as a going concern all the undertaking and assets owned by the Vendor in connection with the

_____
        (type of business)

business carried on as_____
                            (name of business)

at _____
        (address)

(the "business") including, without limiting the generality of the foregoing:

   a) the furniture, fixtures, and equipment more particularly described in Schedule A (the "equipment");

   b) all saleable stock in trade (the "stock in trade");

   c) all useable parts and supplies (the "parts and supplies");

   d) all leasehold interest in the lease held by the Vendor from _____
                                                                    (name of landlord)
       (the "lease");

   e) the goodwill of the business together with the exclusive right to the Purchaser to represent itself as carrying on business in succession to the Vendor and to use the business style of the business and variations in the business to be carried on by the Purchaser (the "goodwill").

1.02 The following assets are expressly excluded from the purchase and sale:

PURCHASE PRICE

2.01 The purchase price payable for the undertaking and assets agreed to be bought and sold is the total of the amounts computed and allocated as follows:

    a) for the equipment — \$ _____ ;

    b) for the stock in trade, its direct cost to the Vendor;

    c) for the parts and supplies, their direct cost to the Vendor;

    d) for the goodwill — \$ _____ ;

    e) for all other assets agreed to be bought and sold — \$1.

2.02 The purchase price for the stock in trade shall be established by an inventory taken and valued after close of business on the day before the day of closing. The Vendor shall produce evidence satisfactory to the Purchaser of the direct cost to the Vendor of items included in stock in trade. The Purchaser may exclude from the purchase and sale any items which the Purchaser reasonably considers unsaleable by reason of defect in quality or in respect of which the Purchaser is not reasonably satisfied as to proof of direct cost.

2.03 The purchase price for the parts and supplies shall be established by an inventory taken and valued after close of business on the day before the day of closing. The Vendor shall produce evidence satisfactory to the Purchaser of the direct cost to the Vendor of items included in the parts and supplies. The Purchaser may exclude from the purchase and sale any items which the Purchaser reasonably considers unuseable or in respect of which the Purchaser is not reasonably satisfied as to proof of direct cost.

TERMS OF PAYMENT

3.01 The Vendor acknowledges receiving a cheque for \$ _____ from the Purchaser on execution of this agreement to be held as a deposit by the Vendor on account of the purchase price of the undertaking and assets agreed to be bought and sold and as security for the Purchaser's due performance of this agreement.

3.02 The balance of the purchase price for the undertaking and assets agreed to be bought and sold shall be paid, subject to adjustments, by certified cheque on closing.

3.03 The balance of the purchase price due on closing shall be specially adjusted for all prepaid and assumed operating expenses of the business including but not limited to rent and utilities.

CONDITIONS, REPRESENTATIONS, AND WARRANTIES

4.01 In addition to anything else in this agreement, the following are conditions of completing this agreement in favour of the Purchaser:

    a) that the Purchaser obtain financing on terms satisfactory to it to complete the purchase;

    b) that the carrying on of the business at its present location is not prohibited by land use restrictions;

    c) that the lessor of the lease consents to its assignment to the Purchaser;

    d) that the Purchaser obtain all the permits and licences required for it to carry on the business;

    e) that the Vendor supply or deliver on closing all of the closing documents.

4.02 The following representations and warranties are made and given by the Vendor to the Purchaser and expressly survive the closing of this agreement. The representations are true as of the date of this agreement and will be true as of the date of closing when they shall continue as warranties according to their terms. At the option of the Purchaser, the representations and warranties may be treated as conditions of the closing of this agreement in favor of the Purchaser. However, the closing of this agreement shall not operate as a waiver or otherwise result in a merger to deprive the Purchaser of the right to sue the Vendor for breach of warranty in respect of any matter warranted, whether or not ascertained by the Purchaser prior to closing:

a) the Vendor is a resident of Canada within the meaning of the Income Tax Act of Canada;

b) the Vendor owns and has the right to sell the items listed in Schedule A;

c) the assets agreed to be bought and sold are sold free and clear of all liens, encumbrances, and charges;

d) the equipment is in good operating condition;

e) the undertaking and assets agreed to be bought and sold will not be adversely affected in any material respect in any way, whether by the Vendor or by any other person or cause whatsoever, up to closing and the Vendor will carry on business as usual until closing and not do anything before or after closing to prejudice the goodwill;

f) the financial statements for the business produced by the Vendor and appended as Schedule B are fair and accurate and prepared in accordance with generally accepted accounting principles;

g) the lease is in good standing and the Vendor has fulfilled all of its obligations under the lease;

h) the Vendor has made full and fair disclosure in all material respects of any matter that could reasonably be expected to affect the Purchaser's decision to purchase the undertaking and assets agreed to be bought and sold on the terms set out in this agreement;

i) the Vendor will execute such assignments, consents, clearances or assurances after closing, prepared at the Purchaser's expense, as the Purchaser considers necessary or desirable to assure the Purchaser of the proper and effective completion of this agreement.

RISK

5.01 The risk of loss or damage to the undertaking and assets agreed to be bought and sold remains with the Vendor until closing.

5.02 In the event of loss or damage to the tangible assets agreed to be bought and sold prior to closing, at the option of the Purchaser, the replacement cost of the assets lost or damaged or any of them may be deducted from the total purchase price otherwise payable by the Purchaser under this agreement and the corresponding lost or damaged assets shall be excluded from the purchase and sale.

SALES TAXES

6.01 The Purchaser shall pay any and all sales taxes payable in respect of the purchase and sale of assets pursuant to this agreement.

6.02 The Vendor shall pay all sales taxes payable or collectible in connection with carrying on the business up to closing and obtain and supply the Purchaser with satisfactory proof of payment within a reasonable time of closing.

NON-COMPETITION

7.01 The Vendor covenants with the Purchaser that, in consideration of the closing of this agreement, the Vendor will not operate a_____

(type of business)

business or in any way aid and assist any other person to operate such a business in _____

_____

(geographical area)

for a period of _____from the date of closing.

BULK SALES

8.01 This agreement shall be completed and the Vendor agrees to comply with any applicable laws governing the sale in bulk of the stock in trade or of any of the other assets pursuant to this agreement.

CLOSING DOCUMENTS

9.01 The Vendor shall deliver to the Purchaser, in registrable form where applicable, the following closing documents (the "closing documents,") prepared or obtained at the Vendor's expense, on or before closing:

a) duplicate, properly executed Bills of Sale of the equipment, stock in trade, and parts and supplies together with evidence satisfactory to the Purchaser that the sale complies with any laws governing the sale in bulk of the stock in trade or of the sale of any of the other assets pursuant to this agreement;

b) a statutory declaration that the Vendor is a resident of Canada within the meaning of the Income Tax Act of Canada as of the date of closing;

c) all records and financial data, including but not limited to any list of customers and suppliers, relevant to the continuation of the business by the Purchaser;

d) a duly executed notice in proper form revoking any registration of the style of the business under any business name registration law;

e) an executed assignment of the lease to the Purchaser endorsed with the lessor's consent to the assignment;

f) such other assignments, consents, clearances, or assurances as the Purchaser reasonably considers necessary or desirable to assure the Purchaser of the proper and effective completion to this agreement.

CLOSING DATE

10.01 The purchase and sale in this agreement shall close on _____.

(date)

MISCELLANEOUS

11.01 In this agreement, the singular includes the plural and the masculine includes the feminine and neuter and vice versa unless the context otherwise requires.

11.02 The capitalized headings in this agreement are only for convenience of reference and do not form part of or affect the interpretation of this agreement.

11.03 If any provision or part of any provision in this agreement is void for any reason, it shall be severed without affecting the validity of the balance of the agreement.

11.04 Time is of the essence of this agreement.

11.05 There are no representations, warranties, conditions, terms, or collateral contracts affecting the transaction contemplated in this agreement except as set out in this agreement.

11.06 This agreement binds and benefits the parties and their respective heirs, executors, administrators, personal representatives, successors, and assigns.

11.07 This agreement is governed by the laws of the Province/Territory of _____.

ACCEPTANCE

12.01 This agreement executed on behalf of the Purchaser constitutes an offer to purchase which can only be accepted by the Vendor by return of at least one originally accepted copy of agreement to the Purchaser on or before _____, failing which, the offer becomes null and void. If this offer becomes null and void or is validly revoked before acceptance or this agreement is not completed by the Purchaser for any valid reason, any deposit tendered with it on behalf of the Purchaser shall be returned without penalty or interest.

Executed under seal on _____.

(date)

Signed, sealed, and   )
delivered in the presence   )
of:)
)

_____) _____ s
for the Purchaser   )   Purchaser
)

_____) _____ s
for the Vendor   )   Vendor

AGREEMENT OF PURCHASE AND SALE OF BUSINESS ASSETS
(WITH LIMITED WARRANTIES)

This agreement of purchase and sale is made in two original copies between

(1)_____

(the "Vendor")

and

(2)_____

(the "Purchaser")

SUBJECT MATTER

1.01 The Purchaser agrees to buy and the Vendor agrees to sell to the Purchaser as a going concern all the undertaking and assets owned by the Vendor in connection with the

_____

(type of business)

business carried on as_____

(name of business)

at _____

(address)

(the "business") including, without limiting the generality of the foregoing:

a) the furniture, fixtures, and equipment more particularly described in Schedule A (the "equipment");

b) all saleable stock in trade (the "stock in trade");

c) all useable parts and supplies (the "parts and supplies");

d) all leasehold interest in the lease held by the Vendor from _____

(name of landlord)

(the "lease");

e) the goodwill of the business together with the exclusive right to the Purchaser to represent itself as carrying on business in succession to the Vendor and to use the business style of the business and variations in the business to be carried on by the Purchaser (the "goodwill").

1.02 The following assets are expressly excluded from the purchase and sale:

PURCHASE PRICE

2.01 The purchase price payable for the undertaking and assets agreed to be bought and sold is the total of the amounts computed and allocated as follows:

a) for the equipment — $ _____;

b) for the stock in trade, its direct cost to the Vendor;

c) for the parts and supplies, their direct cost to the Vendor;

d) for the goodwill — $ _____;

e) for all other assets agreed to be bought and sold — $1.

2.02 The purchase price for the stock in trade shall be established by an inventory taken and valued after close of business on the day before the day of closing. The Vendor shall produce evidence satisfactory to the Purchaser of the direct cost to the Vendor of items included in stock in trade. The Purchaser may exclude from the purchase and sale any items which the Purchaser reasonably considers unsaleable by reason of defect in quality or in respect of which the Purchaser is not reasonably satisfied as to proof of direct cost.

2.03 The purchase price for the parts and supplies shall be established by an inventory taken and valued after close of business on the day before the day of closing. The Vendor shall produce evidence satisfactory to the Purchaser of the direct cost to the Vendor of items included in the parts and supplies. The Purchaser may exclude from the purchase and sale any items which the Purchaser reasonably considers unuseable or in respect of which the Purchaser is not reasonably satisfied as to proof of direct cost.

TERMS OF PAYMENT

3.01 The Vendor acknowledges receiving a cheque for $ _____ from the Purchaser on execution of this agreement to be held as a deposit by the Vendor on account of the purchase price of the undertaking and assets agreed to be bought and sold and as security for the Purchaser's due performance of this agreement. If this agreement is not completed by the Purchaser for any valid reason, the deposit shall be returned without penalty or interest.

3.02 The balance of the purchase price paid for the undertaking and assets agreed to be bought and sold shall be paid, subject to adjustments, by certified cheque on closing.

3.03 The balance of the purchase price due on closing shall be specially adjusted for all prepaid and assumed operating expenses of the business including but not limited to rent and utilities.

CONDITIONS, REPRESENTATIONS, AND WARRANTIES

4.01 The following are conditions of completing this agreement in favour of the Purchaser:

a) that the Vendor owns and has the right to sell the items listed in Schedule A;

b) that the assets agreed to be bought and sold are sold free and clear of all liens, encumbrances and charges;

c) that the carrying on of the business at its present location is not prohibited by land use restrictions;

d) that the lessor of the lease consents to its assignment to the Purchaser;

e) that the lease is in good standing and the Vendor has fulfilled all of its obligations under the lease;

f) that the Vendor supply or deliver on closing all of the required closing documents.

4.02 The Purchaser acknowledges that it is buying the equipment as and where is without any representations or warranties as to quality or fitness for purpose.

4.03 The Purchaser further acknowledges that any representations, warranties, and conditions made or given by the Vendor in connection with this agreement operate only as conditions of closing this agreement and do not survive the closing of this agreement.

RISK

5.01 The risk of loss or damage to the undertaking and assets agreed to be bought and sold remains with the Vendor until closing.

SALES TAX

6.01 The Purchaser shall pay any and all sales taxes payable in respect of the purchase and sale of assets pursuant to this agreement.

BULK SALES

7.01 This agreement shall be completed and the Vendor agrees to comply with any applicable laws governing the sale in bulk of the stock in trade or of any of the other assets pursuant to this agreement.

CLOSING DOCUMENTS

8.01 The Vendor shall deliver to the Purchaser, in registrable form where applicable, the following closing documents, prepared or obtained at the Vendor's expense, on or before closing:

a) duplicate, properly executed Bills of Sale of the equipment, stock in trade, and parts and supplies together with evidence satisfactory to the Purchaser that the sale complies with any laws governing the sale in bulk of the stock in trade or of the sale of any of the other assets pursuant to this agreement;

b) a statutory declaration that the Vendor is a resident of Canada within the meaning of the Income Tax Act of Canada as of the date of closing;

c) any lists of customers and suppliers relevant to the continuation of the business by the Purchaser;

d) a duly executed notice in proper form revoking any registration of the style of the business under any business name registration law;

e) an executed assignment of the lease to the Purchaser endorsed with the lessor's consent to the assignment.

CLOSING DATE

9.01 The purchase and sale in this agreement shall close on_____.
(date)

MISCELLANEOUS

10.01 In this agreement, the singular includes the plural and the masculine includes the feminine and neuter and vice versa unless the context otherwise requires.

10.02 The capitalized headings in this agreement are only for convenience of reference and do not form part of or affect the interpretation of this agreement.

10.03 If any provision or part of any provision in this agreement is void for any reason, it shall be severed without affecting the validity of the balance of the agreement.

10.04 Time is of the essence of this agreement.

10.05 There are no representations, warranties, conditions, terms, or collateral contracts affecting the transaction contemplated in this agreement except as set out in this agreement.

10.06 This agreement binds and benefits the parties and their respective heirs, executors, administrators, personal representatives, successors, and assigns.

10.07 This agreement is governed by the laws of the Province/Territory of _____.

Executed under seal on _____.
(date)

Signed, sealed, and   )
delivered in the presence)
of:)
)
_____)   _____ s
for the Purchaser)   Purchaser
)
_____)   _____ s
for the Vendor)   Vendor

AGREEMENT OF PURCHASE AND SALE OF SHARES

This agreement of purchase and sale is made in two original copies between

(1)_____
(the "Vendor")

and

(2)_____
(the "Purchaser")

Whereas the Vendor owns all of the issued shares of

_____
(the "Corporation");

It is agreed as follows:

SUBJECT MATTER

1.01 The Purchaser agrees to buy and the Vendor agrees to sell to the Purchaser all of the shares owned by the Vendor in the Corporation (the "Shares").

PURCHASE PRICE

2.01 The purchase price payable for the Shares is the total of the amounts allocated among the Shares as follows:

a) for all the (class) _____shares — $ _____

b) for all the (class) _____shares — $ _____etc.

TERMS OF PAYMENT

3.01 The Vendor acknowledges receiving a cheque for $ _____ from the Purchaser on execution of this agreement to be held by the Vendor as a deposit on account of the purchase price of the Shares and as security for the Purchaser's due performance of this agreement.

3.02 The Purchaser shall pay the balance of the purchase price of the Shares by certified cheque on closing.

3.03 It is understood and agreed that the purchase price of the Shares is based on the financial position of the Corporation shown in the balance sheet produced by the Vendor for the Corporation and appended as Schedule A. If the net book value of the Corporation as of the date of closing is less than _____% of the net book value of the Corporation shown in Schedule A, the Vendor shall refund the Purchaser the dollar value difference within a reasonable time of receipt of written notice of the difference. For the purposes of this paragraph, the net book value of the Corporation means the dollar book value of the assets of the Corporation minus the dollar book value of the liabilities, other than for shareholder equity, of the Corporation determined in accordance with generally accepted accounting principles.

CONDITIONS, REPRESENTATIONS, AND WARRANTIES

4.01 In addition to anything else in this agreement, the following are conditions of completing this agreement in favour of the Purchaser:

a) that the Vendor owns all the issued shares of the Corporation;

b) that the Shares are fully paid-up and non-assessable;

c) that no agreement or option exists pursuant to which the Corporation is or may be obliged to issue further shares of its authorized capital;

d) that the Shares are sold free and clear of all liens, encumbrances, and charges;

e) that any consent required for the transfer of the Shares in accordance with the Purchaser's direction is given;

f) that the Corporation is duly incorporated, validly subsisting, and in good standing under the laws of its jurisdiction of incorporation;

g) that the Corporation is not party to any collective agreement with a labour union;

h) that the Vendor give the Purchaser and all duly authorized representatives of the Purchaser full and complete access during normal business hours to the business premises and corporate, business, accounting, tax, and employment records of the Corporation for the purpose of investigating the business and affairs of the Corporation;

i) that the Purchaser obtain financing on terms satisfactory to the Purchaser to complete the purchase;

j) that the Vendor supply or deliver on closing all of the closing documents.

4.02 The Purchaser agrees that, unless and until the purchase of the Shares contemplated in this agreement is completed, the Purchaser shall keep confidential all information obtained by the Purchaser from the Vendor or the Corporation about the Vendor and the business and affairs of the Corporation.

4.03 The following representations and warranties are made and given by the Vendor to the Purchaser and expressly survive the closing of this agreement. The representations are true as of the date of this agreement and will be true as of the date of closing when they shall continue as warranties according to their terms. At the option of the Purchaser, the representations and warranties may be treated as conditions of the closing of this agreement in favor of the Purchaser. However, the closing of this agreement shall not operate as a waiver or otherwise result in a merger to deprive the Purchaser of the right to sue the Vendor for breach of warranty in respect of any matter warranted, whether or not ascertained by the Purchaser prior to closing:

a) the Vendor is a resident of Canada within the meaning of the Income Tax Act of Canada;

b) the Articles of Incorporation and all amendments to the Articles of Incorporation of the Corporation are as stated in Schedule B;

c) the issued share capital of the Corporation is as stated in Schedule C;

d) the balance sheet appended in Schedule A and the financial statements for the last _____ complete fiscal years of the Corporation produced by the Vendor appended
(number)
in Schedule D have been prepared in accordance with generally accepted accounting principles applied on a consistent basis and are fair and accurate;

e) the Corporation owns the assets recorded in the balance sheet appended in Schedule A free and clear of liens, charges, and encumbrances except as noted in Schedule E;

f) the Corporation has properly reported and is not in arrears of payment of any direct or indirect taxes or of any employee-related statutory deductions or remittances;

g) the corporate, business, accounting, tax, and employment records of the Corporation are complete in all material respects;

h) the business of the Corporation will not be adversely affected in any material respect in any way, whether by the Vendor or by any other person or cause whatsoever, up to closing and the Vendor will not do anything before or after closing to prejudice the goodwill of the Corporation;

i) the Corporation will carry on business as usual until closing except that it will not declare any dividends or make any other distributions of capital or retained earnings or undertake or compromise any major contractual liabilities without the express written consent of the Purchaser;

j) there are no outstanding legal actions or judgments against the Corporation and the Corporation is not in default of any agreement to which the Corporation is a party and that all such agreements are in good standing and the Corporation is entitled to all stated benefits in such agreements;

k) the Vendor has made full and fair disclosure in all material respects of any matter that could reasonably be expected to affect the Purchaser's decision to purchase the Shares on the terms set out in this agreement;

l) the Vendor will execute such assignments, consents, clearances, or assurances after closing, prepared at the Purchaser's expense, as the Purchaser considers necessary or desirable to assure the Purchaser of the proper and effective completion of this agreement.

4.04 The following warranty is made and given by the Purchaser to the Vendor in consideration of the closing of this agreement; the Purchaser will personally indemnify and save the Vendor harmless from claims on any outstanding personal guarantees given by the Vendor for the contractual obligations of the Corporation.

NON-COMPETITION

5.01 The Vendor covenants with the Purchaser that, in consideration of the closing of this agreement, the Vendor will not operate a_____
(type of business)
business or in any way aid and assist any other person to operate such a business in _____
_____
(geographical area)
for a period of _____from the date of closing.

CLOSING DOCUMENTS

6.01 The Vendor shall deliver to the Purchaser, in registrable form where applicable, the following closing documents (the "closing documents"), prepared or obtained at the Vendor's expense on or before closing;

a) certificates of the Shares duly assigned in accordance with the direction of the Purchaser together with satisfactory proof of the giving of any consent required for the assignment;

b) all the corporate, business, accounting, tax, and employment records of the Corporation;

c) the written registration of each director and officer of the Corporation effective as of the date of closing together with each director's and officer's personal release of all contracts with and claims against the Corporation;

d) a duly certified record of a resolution passed by the shareholders of the Corporation electing_____
(name(s))

_____

to the Board of Directors of the Corporation effective as of the date of closing;

e) a statutory declaration that the Vendor is a resident of Canada within the meaning of the Income Tax Act of Canada as of the date of closing;

f) such other assignments, consents, clearances, or assurances as the Purchaser reasonably considers necessary or desirable to assure the Purchaser of the proper and effective completion of this agreement.

CLOSING DATE

7.01 The purchase and sale in this agreement shall close on _____.
(date)

MISCELLANEOUS

8.01 In this agreement, the singular includes the plural and the masculine includes the feminine and neuter and vice versa unless the context otherwise requires.

8.02 The capitalized headings in this agreement are only for convenience of reference and do not form part of or affect the interpretation of this agreement.

8.03 If any provision or part of any provision in this agreement is void for any reason, it shall be severed without affecting the validity of the balance of the agreement.

8.04 Time is of the essence of this agreement.

8.05 There are no representations, warranties, conditions, terms, or collateral contracts affecting the transaction contemplated in this agreement except as set out in this agreement.

8.06 This agreement binds and benefits the parties and their respective heirs, executors, administrators, personal representatives, successors, and assigns.

8.07 This agreement is governed by the laws of the Province/Territory of _____.

ACCEPTANCE

9.01 This agreement executed on behalf of the Purchaser constitutes an offer to purchase which can only be accepted by the Vendor by return of at least one originally accepted copy of agreement to the Purchaser on or before_____

(date)

failing which the offer becomes null and void. If this offer becomes null and void or is validly revoked before acceptance or this agreement is not completed by the Purchaser for any valid reason, any deposit tendered with it on behalf of the Purchaser shall be returned without penalty or interest.

Executed under seal on _____.

(date)

Signed, sealed, and	)		
delivered in the presence	)		
of:	)		
	)		
_____	)	_____ s	
for the Purchaser	)	Purchaser	
	)		
_____	)	_____ s	
for the Vendor	)	Vendor	

PARTNERSHIP AGREEMENT

This partnership agreement is made in _____original copies between
(number)

(1)_____
(partner name)

(2)_____
(partner name)

and

(3)_____
(partner name)

(the "Partners").

PARTNERSHIP NAME AND BUSINESS

1.01 The Partners agree to carry on a business of_____
(type of business)

as partners under the name_____.
(the "Partnership")

No person may be introduced as a Partner and no other business may be carried on by the Partnership without the consent in writing of all the Partners.

1.02 The principal place of business of the Partnership for the time being is _____

_____.
(address)

TERM

2.01 The Partnership begins on_____
(date)

and continues until terminated in accordance with this agreement.

PARTNERSHIP SHARES AND CAPITAL

3.01 The Partners shall participate in the assets, liabilities, profits, and losses of the Partnership in the percentages beside their respective names (their "Partnership Shares"):

_____   —   _____ %

_____   —   _____ %

_____   —   _____ %

                                                                          100%

SELF-COUNSEL PRESS—Form 204/04

3.02 The Partners shall contribute a total of $ _____ in cash, in proportion to their respective Partnership Shares, to the start-up capital of the Partnership by no later than _____

_____ .

(date)

3.03 If further capital is required to carry on the Partnership business, the Partners shall contribute it as required in proportion to their respective Partnership Shares.

3.04 No interest accrues on a Partner's capital contributions to the Partnership in proportion to his Partnership Share. However, if a Partner makes an actual payment or advance for the purpose of the Partnership beyond his Partnership Share (an "Additional Advance"), he is entitled to _____% per annum interest from the Partnership on the Additional Advance until refunded by the Partnership.

BANKING ARRANGEMENTS AND FINANCIAL RECORDS

4.01 The Partners shall maintain a bank account in the name of the Partnership business on which cheques may be drawn only on the signature of at least_____of the Partners.

(number)

4.02 The Partners shall at all times maintain full and proper accounts of the Partnership business accessible to each of the Partners at any time on reasonable notice.

PARTNERS' ACCOUNTS AND SALARIES

5.01 The financial records of the Partnership shall include separate income and capital accounts for each Partner.

5.02 No Partner may receive a salary for services rendered to the Partnership but the profit or loss of the Partnership business shall be periodically allocated among the Partners' separate income accounts and each of the Partners may, from time to time, withdraw against a credit balance in his income account.

5.03 The capital accounts of the Partners shall be maintained in proportion to their respective Partnership Shares.

5.04 No Partner shall draw down his capital account without the previous consent in writing of the other Partners. If a Partner draws down his capital account below his Partnership Share, he shall bring it up to his Partnership Share on the demand of any of the Partners.

MANAGEMENT OF PARTNERSHIP BUSINESS

6.01 Each Partner may take part in the management of the Partnership business.

6.02 Any difference arising in the ordinary course of carrying on the Partnership business shall be decided by the Partners having a majority of the Partnership Shares.

PARTNERS' DUTIES AND RESTRICTIONS

7.01 Each Partner shall devote substantially all of his ordinary working time to carrying on the business of the Partnership.

7.02 Each Partner shall at all times duly and punctually pay and discharge his separate debts and liabilities and shall save harmless the property of the Partnership and the other Partners from those separate debts and liabilities and, if necessary, shall promptly indemnify the other Partners for their share of any actual payment or discharge of his separate debts and liabilities by the Partnership.

7.03 No Partner shall assign or encumber his share or interest in the Partnership without the previous consent in writing of the other Partners.

7.04 No Partner shall bind the Partnership or the other Partners for anything outside the ordinary course of carrying on the Partnership business.

FISCAL YEAR END

8.01 The fiscal year end of the Partnership shall be_____in each year.

(month and day)

TERMINATION OF PARTNERSHIP

9.01 The Partnership may be dissolved at any time during the joint lives of the Partners by a Partner giving notice in writing to the other Partners of his intention to dissolve the Partnership, in which case the Partnership is dissolved as from the date mentioned in the notice as the date of dissolution, or, if no date of dissolution is mentioned, as from the date of communication of the notice.

9.02 The Partnership is dissolved on the death or insolvency of any of the Partners or on any of the Partners becoming a mental incompetent so found by a court of law.

9.03 On dissolution of the Partnership, subject to any contrary agreement binding the former Partners and their estates and after making any necessary adjustments in accordance with generally accepted accounting principles to allow for any debit balances in the Partners' separate capital accounts, the Partnership business shall be promptly liquidated and applied in the following order:

a) to pay the debts and liabilities of the Partnership;

b) to refund any outstanding Additional Advances, together with accrued interest;

c) to distribution of the credit balances of the Partners' separate income accounts;

d) to distribution of the credit balances of the Partner's capital accounts;

e) to distribution of any residue to the Partners in proportion to their respective Partnership Shares.

ARBITRATION OF DISPUTES

10.01 Any dispute between the Partners arising out of or related to this agreement and any amendments to it, whether before or after dissolution of the Partnership, shall be referred to and settled by a single arbitrator agreed upon by the Partners or, in default of such agreement, to a single arbitrator appointed pursuant to the legislation governing submissions to arbitration in the jurisdiction whose laws govern this agreement. The decision of the arbitrator is final and binding on the Partners with no right of appeal.

MISCELLANEOUS

11.01 In this agreement, the singular includes the plural and the masculine includes the feminine and neuter and vice versa unless the context otherwise requires.

11.02 The capitalized headings in this agreement are only for convenience of reference and do not form part of or affect the interpretation of this agreement.

11.03 If any provision or part of any provision in this agreement is void for any reason, it shall be severed without affecting the validity of the balance of the agreement.

11.04 Time is of the essence of this agreement.

11.05 The terms of this agreement may only be amended in writing dated and signed by all the Partners.

11.06 This agreement binds and benefits the Partners and their respective heirs, executors, administrators, personal representatives, successors, and assigns.

11.07 This agreement is governed by the laws of the Province/Territory of _____.

Executed under seal on_____ .
                                            (date)

Signed, sealed and   )
delivered in the presence   )
of:)
_____   )   _____s
)   *(Partner signature)*
)
_____   )   _____s
)   *(Partner signature)*
)
_____   )   _____s
)   *(Partner signature)*

JOINT VENTURE AGREEMENT

This joint venture agreement is made in _____ original copies between
(number)

(1)_____
(Joint Venture Partner name)

(2)_____
(Joint Venture Partner name)

and

(3)_____
(Joint Venture Partner name)

(the "Joint Venture Partners").

PARTNERSHIP BUSINESS

1.01 The Joint Venture Partners agree to carry on a joint venture with regard to

_____

_____

_____
(description of venture)

as partners (the "Partnership"). No person may be introduced as a Joint Venture Partner and no other business may be carried on by the Partnership without the consent in writing of all the Joint Venture Partners.

TERM

2.01 The Partnership begins on_____and continues
(date)

until terminated in accordance with this agreement.

PARTNERSHIP SHARES AND CAPITAL

3.01 The Joint Venture Partners shall participate in the assets, liabilities, profits, and losses of the Partnership in the percentages beside their respective names (their "Partnership Shares"):

_____ — _____ %

_____ — _____ %

_____ — _____ %

100%

3.02 The Joint Venture Partners shall contribute a total of $ _____in cash, in proportion to their respective Partnership Shares, to the start-up capital of the Partnership by no later than _____.
(date)

3.03 No interest accrues on a Joint Venture Partner's capital contributions to the Partnership in proportion to his Partnership Share. However, if a Joint Venture Partner makes an actual payment or advance for the purpose of the Partnership beyond his Partnership Share (an "Additional Advance"), he is entitled to _____% per annum interest from the Partnership on the Additional Advance until refunded by the Partnership.

SELF-COUNSEL PRESS—Form 205/04

BANKING ARRANGEMENTS AND FINANCIAL RECORDS

4.01 The Partnership shall maintain a bank account on which cheques may be drawn only on the signature of the Managing Joint Venture Partner (see below) or the signatures of all the Joint Venture Partners.

4.02 The Partnership shall at all times maintain full and proper accounts of the Partnership business accessible to each of the Joint Venture Partners at any time on reasonable notice.

PARTNERS' ACCOUNTS AND SALARIES

5.01 The financial records of the Partnership shall include separate income and capital accounts for each Joint Venture Partner.

5.02 No Joint Venture Partner may receive a salary for services rendered to the Partnership but the profit or loss of the Partnership business shall be periodically allocated among the Joint Venture Partners' separate income accounts and each of the Joint Venture Partners may, from time to time, withdraw against a credit balance in his income account.

5.03 The capital accounts of the Joint Venture Partners shall be maintained in proportion to their respective Partnership Shares.

5.04 No Joint Venture Partner shall draw down his capital account without the previous consent in writing of the other Joint Venture Partners. If a Joint Venture Partner draws down his capital account below his Partnership Share of all the Joint Venture Partners' capital accounts, he shall bring it up to his Partnership Share on the demand of any of the Joint Venture Partners.

MANAGEMENT OF PARTNERSHIP BUSINESS

6.01 The management of the Partnership business is vested in a Managing Joint Venture Partner elected and removable by a majority vote of the Joint Venture Partners in the Partnership.

6.02 The Managing Joint Venture Partner is not liable to the Joint Venture Partners or the Partnership for any acts or failures to act in the course of managing the Partnership business committed in good faith.

PARTNERS' DUTIES AND RESTRICTION

7.01 Each Joint Venture Partner shall at all times duly and punctually pay and discharge his separate debts and liabilities and shall save harmless the property of the Partnership and the other Joint Venture Partners from those separate debts and liabilities and, if necessary, shall promptly indemnify the other Joint Venture Partners for their share of any actual payment or discharge of his separate debts and liabilities by the Partnership.

7.02 No Joint Venture Partner shall assign or encumber his share or interest in the Partnership without the previous consent in writing of the other Joint Venture Partners.

7.03 No Joint Venture Partner shall bind the Partnership or the other Joint Venture Partners for anything outside the ordinary course of carrying on the Partnership business.

TERMINATION OF PARTNERSHIP

8.01 The Partnership may only be voluntarily dissolved during the joint lives of the Joint Venture Partners by mutual agreement of the Joint Venture Partners.

8.02 On voluntary dissolution of the Partnership, subject to any contrary agreement binding the former Joint Venture Partners and after making any necessary adjustments in accordance with generally accepted accounting principles to allow for any debit balances in the Joint Venture Partners' separate capital accounts, the Partnership business shall be promptly liquidated and applied in the following order:

a) to pay the debts and liabilities of the Partnership;

b) to refund any outstanding Additional Advances, together with accrued interest;

c) to distribution of the credit balances of the Joint Venture Partners' separate income accounts;

d) to distribution of the credit balances of the Joint Venture partners' separate capital accounts;

e) to distribution of any residue to the Joint Venture Partners in proportion to their respective Partnership Shares.

8.03 A Joint Venture Partner involuntarily ceases to be a Joint Venture Partner on death or insolvency or becoming a mental incompetent so found by a court of law but the Partnership continues.

8.04 On a Joint Venture Partner involuntarily ceasing to be a Joint Venture Partner, subject to any contrary agreement binding the former Joint Venture Partner and the remaining Joint Venture Partners and after making any necessary adjustments in accordance with generally accepted accounting principles to allow for any debt balances in the Joint Venture Partners' separate capital accounts, the remaining Joint Venture Partners shall pay the Joint Venture Partner ceasing to be a Joint Venture Partner or his estate, as the case may be, any credit balances in his separate income and capital accounts as shown on the financial statements of the Partnership for the next month end following the date of his ceasing to be a Joint Venture Partner (the "Payment Calculation Statements") and, upon payment, the Joint Venture Partner ceasing to be a Joint Venture Partner has no further claims against the Partnership or the remaining Joint Venture Partners in respect of his interest in the Partnership. For greater certainty, the Payment Calculation Statements shall not be adjusted to show a value for goodwill or work-in-progress but shall be adjusted as though for a fiscal year end.

ARBITRATION OF DISPUTES

9.01 Any dispute between the Joint Venture Partners arising out of or related to this agreement and any amendments to it, whether before or after dissolution of the Partnership or a Joint Venture Partner involuntarily ceases to be a Joint Venture Partner, shall be referred to and settled by a single arbitrator appointed pursuant to the legislation governing submissions to arbitration in the province whose laws govern this agreement. The decision of the arbitrator is final and binding on the Joint Venture Partners with no right of appeal.

MISCELLANEOUS

10.01 In this agreement, the singular includes the plural and the masculine includes the feminine and neuter and vice versa unless the context otherwise requires.

10.02 The capitalized headings in this agreement are only for convenience of reference and do not form part of or affect the interpretation of this agreement.

10.03 If any provision or part of any provision in this agreement is void for any reason, it shall be severed without affecting the validity of the balance of the agreement.

10.04 Time is of the essence of this agreement.

10.05 The terms of this agreement may only be amended in writing dated and signed by all the Joint Venture Partners.

10.06 This agreement binds and benefits the Joint Venture Partners and their respective heirs, executors, administrators, personal representatives, successors, and assigns.

10.07 This agreement is governed by the laws of the Province/Territory of _____.

Executed under seal on _____.
                                                    (date)

Signed, sealed, and   )
delivered in the presence   )
of:)
)
_____   )   _____s
)   *(Joint Venture Partner signature)*
)
_____   )   _____s
)   *(Joint Venture Partner signature)*
)
_____   )   _____s
)   *(Joint Venture Partner signature)*

PARTNERSHIP AGREEMENT CHECKLIST

1.   Name of Partnership

_____

2.   Names of Partners

_____

_____

_____

_____

_____

_____

3.   Description of Business

_____

_____

_____

_____

4.   Commencement Date

_____

5.   Term of Partnership (if any)

_____

6.   Place of Business (if any)

_____

_____

7. Contributions to Capital

_____

_____

_____

_____

8. Division of Profits

_____

_____

_____

_____

9. Fiscal Year-end

_____

10. Accounting/Valuation Principles (seek professional advice)

_____

_____

_____

_____

11. Banking Arrangements

_____

12. Management Duties/Decisions

_____

_____

_____

13.   Restrictions on Partners

_____

_____

_____

14.   Signing Authority

_____

_____

15.   Drawing Arrangements

_____

_____

16.   Retirement/Death Arrangements

_____

_____

17.   Non-Competition Clause?

_____

_____

18.   Admission/Expulsion of Partners

_____

_____

19.   Voluntary Dissolution of Partnership

_____

_____

20.   Dispute Arbitration Clause?

_____

_____

_____

DISTRIBUTION AGREEMENT

This distribution agreement is made in three original copies between

(1)_____

(the "Supplier")

and

(2)_____

(the "Distributor")

and is personally guaranteed by

(3)_____

(the "Guarantor")

Whereas the Supplier wishes to market the products described in Schedule A (the "Products") through the Distributor;

It is agreed as follows:

DISTRIBUTION RIGHTS

1.01 The Supplier grants the Distributor an exclusive right to sell the Products within the territory described in Schedule B for a period of _____
commencing _____ (the "Distribution Rights").
(date)

1.02 The Distributor shall pay the Supplier a non-refundable fee of _____dollars ($ _____) on signing this agreement for the initial grant of the Distribution Rights.

1.03 The Distributor shall not sell or attempt to sell the Products outside of the territory described in Schedule B.

1.04 The Distributor shall use its best efforts to sell the Products for the duration of the Distribution Rights.

1.05 The Distributor may describe itself as an authorized distributor of the Products for the duration of the Distribution Rights but shall not characterize itself or enter into any transaction as an agent or in the name of the Supplier.

PRODUCT PRICES

2.01 The Supplier shall supply the Distributor with Products on the Distributor's order at the price(s), inclusive of cost of delivery to the Supplier at_____

_____

(address)

set out in Schedule C. For greater certainty, the price(s) set out in Schedule C are quoted exclusive of any taxes and duties payable in connection with the sale which, if payable by the Supplier, may be added by the Supplier to the cost of the Products to the Distributor.

2.02 The Distributor shall pay the Supplier for the Products ordered from the Supplier

_____

_____

_____

_____

(terms of payment)

2.03 The Distributor may re-sell the Products at whatever price(s) the Distributor sees fit.

DEFECTIVE PRODUCTS

3.01 The Distributor may return all defective Products to the Supplier for replacement at the Supplier's expense.

3.02 The Supplier agrees to indemnify the Distributor against third-party liability incurred by selling defective Products but only to the extent that the Distributor could not have avoided or minimized the liability or damages by exercising reasonable care not to sell defective Products.

TRAINING

4.01 At the request of the Distributor, the Supplier shall train the Distributor's employees, at the Supplier's place of business and at the expense of the Distributor, in the proper use of the Products. The Supplier shall not charge the Distributor in excess of _____
dollars ($ _____) per hour of Supplier employee time for training the Distributor's employees.

ADVERTISING AND INFORMATION MATERIALS

5.01 For the duration of the Distribution Rights, the Supplier shall furnish the Distributor, at the Supplier's cost, with reasonable quantities of advertising and user information materials to aid the Distributor in selling the Products.

PRODUCT IMAGE

6.01 Other than in the matter of pricing, the Distributor shall not do or permit anything to be done to prejudice the market image of the Products or the Supplier.

RESTRAINT OF COMPETITION

7.01 The Distributor shall not sell, or in any way assist anyone else to sell, any products that compete with the Products of the Supplier within the territory described in Schedule B for the duration of the Distribution Rights and for the calendar year immediately following termination of the Distribution Rights.

7.02 The Guarantor shall not sell, or in any way assist anyone else to sell, any products that compete with the Products of the Supplier within the territory described in Schedule B for the duration of the Distribution Rights and for the calendar year immediately following termination of the Distribution Rights.

SUMMARY TERMINATION OF DISTRIBUTION RIGHTS

8.01 If the Distributor breaks any term of this agreement, the Supplier may summarily terminate the Distribution Rights on notice in writing to the Distributor.

TERMINATION CONSEQUENCES

9.01 On termination of the Distribution Rights for any reason, the Distributor shall immediately cease to describe itself as an authorized distributor of the Supplier and, at the Supplier's option, the Supplier may buy back the Distributor's unsold Products or any part of them at the Distributor's cost.

ASSIGNMENT

10.01 The Distributor shall not assign the benefit of this agreement or subcontract its obligations under this agreement without the consent in writing of the Supplier, which consent may be withheld without good reason.

GUARANTEE

11.01 The Guarantor guarantees the Supplier the due performance of this agreement by the Distributor.

MISCELLANEOUS

12.01 In this agreement, the singular includes the plural and the masculine includes the feminine and neuter and vice versa unless the context otherwise requires.

12.02 The capitalized headings in this agreement are only for convenience of reference and do not form part of or affect the interpretation of this agreement.

12.03 If any provision or part of any provision in this agreement is void for any reason, it shall be severed without affecting the validity of the balance of the agreement.

12.04 Time is of the essence of this agreement.

12.05 There are no representations, warranties, conditions, terms or collateral contracts affecting the transaction contemplated in this agreement except as set out in this agreement.

12.06 Nothing in this agreement is intended to constitute a partnership between any of the parties.

12.07 This agreement binds and benefits the parties and their respective heirs, executors, administrators, personal representatives, successors, and assigns.

12.08 This agreement is governed by the laws of the Province/Territory of _____.

Executed under seal on_____
(date)

_____
(supplier corporate name)

per:_____ c/s
(signer's name, office)

_____
(distributor corporate name)

per:_____ c/s
(signer's name, office)

Signed, sealed, and)	
delivered in the presence)	
of:)	
)	
_____)	_____s
for the Guarantor)	*(Guarantor signature)*

COMMISSION SALES AGREEMENT

This commission sales agreement is made in two original copies between

(1)_____

and

(2)_____

Whereas the Principal wishes to market the product(s) described in Schedule A (the "Product(s)");

And whereas the Agent is prepared to sell the Product(s) on behalf of the Principal in return for a commission;

It is agreed as follows:

SELLING RIGHTS

1.01 The Principal grants the Agent an exclusive right to sell the Product(s) on behalf of the Principal within the territory described in Schedule B for a period of _____ commencing _____ (the "Selling Rights").
(date)

1.02 The Agent may not sell or attempt to sell the Product(s) outside of the territory described in Schedule B.

1.03 The Agent shall use his best efforts to sell the Product(s) for the duration of the Selling Rights. At the request from time to time of the Principal, the Agent shall furnish the Principal with a reasonably detailed, written report on his efforts to sell the Product(s) in the period specified by the Principal.

1.04 The Agent shall clearly identify himself as a duly authorized sales agent of the Principal in the course of his efforts to sell the Product(s) on behalf of the Principal and may not sell the Product(s) in his own name.

PRODUCT PRICES

2.01 The Principal shall fix the selling price(s) of the Product(s) and the Agent may only sell the Product(s) at the selling price(s) fixed by the Principal.

ORDERS

3.01 The Agent shall obtain written orders for the Product(s) from buyers, signed by or on behalf of the buyers, and remit the orders to the Principal.

3.02 The Principal shall use its best efforts to fill orders duly remitted by the Agent in accordance with this agreement as expeditiously as possible.

COMMISSION

4.01 The Principal shall pay the Agent a commission of _____% of the selling price, exclusive of any sales taxes, of each order or part of each order of Product(s) duly remitted by the Agent in accordance with this agreement which is paid for in full, inclusive of any sales taxes, and which is not subsequently returned for a refund.

4.02 The Principal may accept the return of Product(s) for a refund or partial refund in its sole discretion.

4.03 The Agent is not entitled to any compensation for services performed or expenses incurred in connection with this agreement other than as set out in this agreement.

TRAINING

5.01 At the request of the Agent, the Principal shall train the Agent in the proper use of the Product(s).

ADVERTISING AND INFORMATION MATERIALS

6.01 For the duration of the Selling Rights, the Principal shall furnish the Agent, at the Principal's cost, with reasonable quantities of advertising and user information materials, including demonstration Product(s), to aid the Agent in selling the Product(s).

PRODUCT IMAGE

7.01 The Agent shall not do or permit anything to be done to prejudice the market image of the Product(s) or the Principal.

RESTRAINT OF COMPETITION

8.01 The Agent shall not sell, or in any way assist anyone else to sell, any products that compete with the Product(s) of the Principal within the territory described in Schedule B for the duration of the Selling Rights and for the calendar year immediately following termination of the Selling Rights.

CONFIDENTIALITY

9.01 The Agent shall keep the Principal's business secrets, including but not limited to customer, supplier, logistical, financial, research, and development information, confidential and shall not disclose them to any third party during and after termination of the Selling Rights.

SUMMARY TERMINATION OF SELLING RIGHTS

10.01 If the Agent breaks any term of this agreement, the Principal may summarily terminate the Selling Rights on notice in writing to the Agent.

TERMINATION CONSEQUENCES

11.01 On termination of the Selling Rights for any reason, the Agent shall immediately cease to describe himself as an authorized sales agent of the Principal and cease selling the Product(s).

ASSIGNMENT

12.01 The Agent shall not assign the benefit of this agreement or subcontract his obligations under this agreement without the consent in writing of the Principal, which consent may be withheld without good reason.

FIDUCIARY RELATIONSHIP

13.01 The Agent accepts and acknowledges that the terms of this agreement are in addition to and do not detract from the ordinary fiduciary duties owed by the Agent to the Principal.

MISCELLANEOUS

14.01 In this agreement, the singular includes the plural and the masculine includes the feminine and neuter and vice versa unless the context otherwise requires.

14.02 The capitalized headings in this agreement are only for convenience of reference and do not form part of or affect the interpretation of this agreement.

14.03 If any provision or part of any provision in this agreement is void for any reason, it shall be severed without affecting the validity of the balance of the agreement.

14.04 Time is of the essence of this agreement.

14.05 There are no representations, warranties, conditions, terms, or collateral contracts affecting the transaction contemplated in this agreement except as set out in this agreement.

14.06 Nothing in this agreement is intended to constitute a partnership or a master and servant relationship between the parties.

14.07 This agreement binds and benefits the parties and their respective heirs, executors, administrators, personal representatives, successors and assigns.

14.08 This agreement is governed by the laws of the Province/Territory of _____.

Executed under seal on _____.
                                    (date)

Signed, sealed, and	)	
delivered in the presence	)	
of:	)	
_____	)	_____s
for the Principal	)	*(Principal signature)*
	)	
_____	)	_____s
for the Agent	)	*(Commission Agent signature)*

BUSINESS PLAN CHECKLIST

A. BACKGROUND

    1. A narrative description of the development of the business or concept including the rationale for entering specific markets.

B. MANAGEMENT

    1. Resumes of the executives and senior supervisory personnel detailing:

        a) age

        b) academic background

        c) shareholdings

        d) functions

        e) accomplishments

        f) business references

        g) current remuneration

    2. Availability of personnel replacements. Define to what extent the plan is dependent on certain people.

    3. Schematic organization chart that describes the responsibilities associated with each major management position.

    4. Identify the timing and need for new management.

C. NON-MANAGEMENT WORKFORCE

    1. Identify the following:

        a) skills required

        b) timing of need for labour

        c) labour availability

        d) compensation levels

    2. Describe the fringe benefit plan and how it compares with other companies in the same geographical area and in the same industry.

    3. Current or anticipated status of union contracts, demands, and objectives with a summary of labour relations within the company. Name current and prospective unions.

    4. Availability of skilled and unskilled labour to meet company objectives.

    5. Describe labour intensity of company and labour turnover.

D. RESEARCH AND DEVELOPMENT

    1. Indicate why the product or process is unique and worthy of financial support.

2. Provide independent support for the product, service, or process including users' reports and endorsements.

3. Comment on the state of the art domestically and internationally.

4. Comment on ability to legally protect know-how and lead time over the competition.

5. Describe anticipated research and development costs to advance prototype to production line or to improve existing production line product.

6. Describe future pressures on research and development including probable product adaptations.

E. MARKETING

1. Describe in detail the existing and proposed products or services. Submit sales literature, photographs, drawings, etc.

2. Describe the customer benefits and advantages over existing competitive products or services.

3. Define the company's marketing philosophy. Outline a detailed marketing plan which would include:

    a) analysis by product by territory

    b) optimal distribution method

    c) price structure including product line profit contribution

    d) break-even analysis by product and territory

    e) market characteristics and market measurement

    f) identification of principal actual and potential customers

    g) product and package testing

    h) test marketing

    i) media selection for marketing

    j) warranty/service policy

4. Provide an analysis of competitors including an evaluation of their products, pricing, and market share.

5. Provide an estimate of market start-up costs for new products.

F. MANUFACTURING

1. Provide a manufacturing plan that will identify:

    a) the need for physical plant

    b) optimal size and layout of plant

    c) capacity of plant

    d) alternative uses

    e) burden of fixed costs and availability of a trade-off of fixed costs for variable costs (i.e., subcontracting component production)

f) cost of the fixed assets required

2. The plan will provide a cost analysis that will include:

    a) complete bill of materials costing, each naming at least two suppliers

    b) price trends of major raw materials compared to trends in selling price of finished products

    c) availability of all major items of raw material

3. The plan will address the following manufacturing standards:

    a) size

    b) weight

    c) durability

    d) convenience

    e) packaging

    f) quality

    g) colour

    h) customer service

    i) product standardization and compatibility

4. Comment on how plant location has been/will be determined including reference to customer proximity, supplier proximity, labour availability, transportation, etc.

5. Describe and diagram the production process.

6. Comment on production planning and scheduling procedures including an estimate of start-up expenses.

7. Briefly describe existing plant and property. Comment on physical condition of plant and equipment including outstanding capital projects and probable costs of expansion.

G. LEGAL

1. Provide incorporation details:

    a) date

    b) jurisdiction

    c) registered office

    d) directors

    e) officers

    f) shareholders

2. Attach copies of the Incorporation Certificate.

3. Provide information on predecessor companies or partnerships including a copy of financial statements and a copy of asset and know-how transfer.

4. Submit a copy of:

   a) employment contracts

   b) pension plans including actuarial reports on extent of unfunded past service liabilities

   c) profit sharing plans

   d) options and warrants

   e) patents, trademarks, industrial designs

   f) franchise and distributorship agreements

5. Provide details on all non-arm's-length relationships.

6. State whether the company's beneficial contracts are assignable. Consider licences, royalty agreements, employment contracts, leases, suppliers' contracts, collective bargaining agreements.

7. Comment on any litigation, actual or contemplated, as well as any changes of law that will affect the company.

8. Describe those aspects of the company's business now subject to government control and regulations.

H. FINANCIAL

1. Actual audited financial statements for the last five years if possible. Transfer to a comparative summary for ease of study.

2. Most recent interim financial statement. Ensure that all appropriate accruals are reflected in the interim.

3. Detailed cash flow and income projections should be provided for the next 36 months. All assumptions should be described. Pro-forma balance sheets should also be prepared.

4. Costs should be broken into fixed and variable components and the break-even point should be determined.

5. Whenever existing loans are outstanding, identify:

   a) lender

   b) terms

   c) balance

   d) security

   e) restrictive covenants

   f) lending officer

3
SERVICES

Form 300. Engagement of services

Use this form to confirm the terms of an oral engagement of your professional or white-collar services by a client/customer. Note that the client/customer agrees to late-payment charges at the time of entering into the contract of engagement (which is required by law) and get a personal guarantee of payment for a corporate client/customer (but only where not likely to offend an established corporation).

Form 301. Engagement of another's services

Use this form to confirm the terms of an oral engagement of someone else's professional or white-collar services by your firm.

Form 302. Independent contractor agreement

Use this form, with proper legal advice, to draft a simple, blue-collar, independent contractor agreement.

Under section 1, insert general description of work.

Form 303. Authorized extras

Use this form in a blue-collar, independent contractor situation to document the authorization of extra work.

Form 304. Change work order

Use this form in a blue-collar, independent contractor situation to document agreed work changes.

ENGAGEMENT OF SERVICES

_____, 20__

Dear _____:

Re Terms of Engagement

This letter confirms our understanding of the terms of our engagement by _____

    A) We will provide the following services: _____

    B) Our charges for these services are: _____

    C) We will bill you: _____

    D) Our invoices are all payable on receipt and bear interest on their unpaid amount at the rate of _____% per annum compounded annually.

    E) If the client is or becomes incorporated, the individual accepting the terms of our engagement on behalf of the client also personally guarantees payment for our services.

Please indicate your agreement to these terms by completing the acceptance on the accompanying copy of this letter and returning it to us.

Yours very truly,

_____
(Signature)

The terms of engagement in this letter are accepted.

_____   )   _____
Date:)   By:

ENGAGEMENT OF ANOTHER'S SERVICES

_____, 20__

Dear _____:

Re Terms of Engagement

This letter confirms our understanding of the terms of engagement of your services by our firm.

A) You will provide the following services:_____

B) You will commence work on _____ and substantially complete it by no
   (date)

later than _____
          (date)

C) Your charges for these services will be:

If the above accords with your understanding of the terms of your engagement, please accept this letter as your authority to start work.

Any variation of the above terms, including the provision of additional services, requires our written consent.

Yours very truly,

_____
(Signature)

INDEPENDENT CONTRACTOR AGREEMENT

This contract for services is made in two original copies between

(1)_____

(the "Hirer")

and

(2)_____

(the "Contractor")

It is agreed as follows:

   1. The Contractor shall provide the Hirer with the following services as an independent contractor:

(the "Work").

   2. The Contractor shall commence the Work on _____ and substantially

(date)

complete it by no later than _____.

(date)

   3. The total contract price (the "Contract Price") payable by the Hirer to the Contractor for doing the Work, exclusive of any Authorized Extras, is _____ dollars

($_____).

   4. Subject to any statutory holdbacks under any applicable construction or mechanics lien legislation, the Hirer shall pay the Contract Price as follows:

_____

_____

(terms and time of payment)

   5. The Contractor is only liable to perform and the Hirer is only liable to pay for extra services, in addition to the Work, that are authorized in writing setting out the price of the extra services and signed by both parties ("Authorized Extras").

   6. The Contractor is entitled to interest at the rate of _____ % per annum on any overdue payments for doing the Work and any Authorized Extras under this agreement.

7. The Contractor shall indemnify and save the Hirer harmless from any and all claims against the Hirer arising out of the performance of the Contractor's services under this agreement.

8. Time is of the essence of this agreement.

9. The terms of this agreement may only be amended in writing signed by both parties.

10. This agreement is governed by the laws of the Province/Territory of _____.

Executed under seal on _____.
                              (date)

Signed, sealed, and   )
delivered in the presence   )
of:)
)
_____   )   _____
for the Hirer   )   *(Hirer signature)*
)
_____   )   _____
for the Contractor   )   *(Contractor signature)*

AUTHORIZED EXTRAS

Project:

Hirer:

Contractor:

Contract Date:

1. The Hirer authorizes and the Contractor agrees to do the following extra work in addition to the work set out in the above dated contract:

2. The agreed total price for the above extra work is _____ dollars ($ _____).

Signed on _____
                            (date)

_____   _____
the Hirer   the Contractor

CHANGE WORK ORDER

Project:

Hirer:

Contractor:

Contract Date:

1. The Hirer authorizes and the Contractor agrees to make the following work changes to the above dated contract:

2. There is no additional charge for the above changes.

OR

2. The agreed additional charge for the above changes is _____ dollars ($_____).

Signed on _____
(date)

_____   _____
the Hirer   the Contractor

4

EMPLOYMENT

Form 400. Rejecting employment application

Use this form to deal with rejected applications for employment with your firm.

Form 401. Confirming employment terms

Use this form to document the terms of an offer of employment in secretarial or junior clerical hiring situation. Note the careful statement of annual cash salary as inclusive of statutory vacation pay and equivalent to a certain sum. When the employee is not entitled to paid vacation, this avoids any confusion as to whether weekly salary is calculated by dividing by 52 weeks or by 52 weeks less 2 weeks' vacation.

Under section b, at the end of the paragraph, list fringe benefits, or, if there are no fringe benefits, insert the following statement: "There are no fringe benefits in connection with your employment, and, in particular, there is no sick leave."

Form 402. Employment agreement

Use this form with proper legal advice to prepare a simple employment contract for more senior employees. Note the firing notice provision to limit damages for wrongful dismissal where the employee is let go or fired without good cause in law. Note also provision for a non-competition clause.

In section 2, insert list of duties in the proper space.

In section 6, list benefits at the end of the paragraph.

In section 8, if the employee is not entitled to sick leave, do not fill in the number of days and the time period; instead, insert the following statement at the end of the paragraph: "It is understood and agreed that the employee is not entitled to any paid or unpaid sick leave."

In section 10, insert type of business, geographical area, and time period in their respective places.

Form 403. Employee warning notice

Generally speaking, you cannot fire someone for incompetence without giving that person fair warning about specific problems and a reasonable opportunity to improve performance. Use this form to document the warning.

Insert description of problems requiring warning notice at the end of the first paragraph.

Insert details of requirements to improve performance at the end of the second paragraph.

Form 404. Employee dismissal notice

Firing an employee for just cause is not to be taken lightly. Use this form, with proper legal advice, to advise the employee of his or her dismissal and give reasons for it. Note that advance notice of dismissal (e.g., at the end of the week or month) or an offer of money in lieu of advance notice of dismissal may be interpreted as a waiver of your right to fire the employee for cause without notice.

Insert details of reasons for termination of employment at the end of the first paragraph.

Form 405. Employee covenants: secrecy/ non-competition

Use this form, with proper legal advice, to protect your firm from employee disclosure of business secrets and departing employee competition. Restraint of competition is void as against public policy unless it is reasonable including as to length of time (e.g., one year) and geographical area (e.g., Regional Municipality of Ottawa-Carleton) of restraint. Reasonableness depends on the circumstances and customs of your industry. As a general rule, do not exceed two years for length of time (this does not mean automatically use two years) or specify a geographical area in excess of your ordinary market operations. Note that we have provided a choice of non-competition clauses, one for general competition and the other specifically for customer account competition.

Insert type of business, geographical area, and time period in their respective places in section 2.

Insert time period in proper place in section 3.

Form 406. Employee covenant: expense recovery

Use this form to obtain an enforceable employee promise to reimburse expenses disallowed as proper deductions by the tax authorities.

Form 407. Employee invention covenant

Use this form to obtain an enforceable employee acknowledgment of an employer's ownership of "employee" inventions.

REJECTING EMPLOYMENT APPLICATION

_____, 20__

Dear _____:

Re Employment Application

Thank you for your employment application.

Unfortunately, we are unable to offer you a position with our firm at this time.

We wish you the best in your search for employment.

Yours very truly,

_____

(Signature)

CONFIRMING EMPLOYMENT TERMS

_____, 20__

Dear _____:

Re Offer of Employment

This is to confirm our offer to you of a position with this firm as a _____
(position)

commencing _____ on the following terms:
(date)

a) You will be on probation for _____ weeks during which time we may terminate your employment at any time without notice or payment in lieu of notice. If your employment is continued, we may only terminate your employment without cause on two weeks' notice or payment in lieu of notice; however, we reserve the right to terminate your employment at any time without notice or payment in lieu of notice for good cause;

b) Your gross cash salary, inclusive of any statutory vacation pay to which you may be entitled, during the probationary period of your employment is equivalent to $_____ per annum payable, subject to statutory deductions, in weekly installments not in advance; if your employment is continued, your gross cash salary, inclusive of any statutory vacation pay to which you may be entitled, will increase to the equivalent of $_____ per annum also payable, subject to statutory deductions, in weekly installments not in advance; in addition, you have the following taxable fringe benefits in connection with your employment:

c) Subject to statutory holidays, your hours of employment are _____ a.m. to _____ p.m., Monday through Friday, with _____ minutes off for lunch and two _____ minute coffee breaks (one to be taken in the morning and the other in the afternoon) each full working day.

SELF-COUNSEL PRESS—Form 401/04

d) You have up to _____ weeks' ordinary vacation each year; you will not receive your ordinary pay while on vacation but you will be paid any statutory vacation pay to which you are entitled; all vacation time must be reserved _____ months in advance; no ordinary vacation may be taken during the first _____ months, including the probationary period, of employment.

e) You may not accumulate your time for lunches, coffee breaks, or ordinary vacation and these must all be scheduled subject to reasonable control over timing by the firm.

f) All overtime must be expressly requested and authorized in advance by the firm; otherwise, it is worked at your own risk.

g) Your employment duties consist of:

however, this list is not to be taken as fixed or exhaustive and you will be expected to perform any reasonable employment task given by a superior.

h) You agree not to disclose any confidential information learned in the course of your employment about the business of the firm or about its clients or about the personal affairs of your superiors to anybody outside the firm both during and after your term of employment.

If this is your understanding of the terms of our offer of employment, please complete the acceptance of employment on the accompanying copy of this letter and return the copy to us. If there is anything with which you do not agree, please feel free to discuss it with the writer.

Welcome to the firm.

Yours very truly,

_____
(Signature)

Employment on the terms set out in this letter is accepted.

_____   _____
Date: By:

SELF-COUNSEL PRESS—Form 401/04

EMPLOYMENT AGREEMENT

This employment agreement is made in two original copies between

(1)_____

(the "Employer")

and

(2)_____

(the "Employee")

It is agreed as follows:

1. The Employer agrees to employ the Employee and the Employee agrees to work for the Employer as a _____

(position)

for an indefinite period of time commencing _____

(date)

2. Subject to reasonable direction by the Employer, the Employee shall perform the following duties and have the following responsibilities:

However, it is understood and agreed that these duties and responsibilities are not exhaustive and may be changed with the Employer's changing circumstances; in this regard, the Employee may not refuse any reasonable employment request by the Employer.

3. Subject to statutory holidays and ordinary vacation, the Employee shall work from _____ a.m. to _____ p.m., Monday through Friday in each week of employment.

4. In addition to statutory holidays, the Employee is entitled to _____ weeks' ordinary, unpaid, non-cumulative vacation in each calendar year of employment but the Employee may not take any ordinary vacation until after _____ months of employment.

5. It is understood and agreed that any ordinary vacation is subject to reasonable control over scheduling by the Employer.

SELF-COUNSEL PRESS—Form 402/04

6. Subject to statutory deductions, the Employer shall pay the Employee a gross cash salary, inclusive of any statutory vacation pay to which the Employee may be entitled, equivalent to _____ dollars ($_____) per annum in weekly installments not in advance. In addition, the Employer shall make the following taxable fringe benefits available to the Employee for the term of employment:

7. The Employer shall also reimburse the Employee for all authorized business expenses incurred by the Employee in the course of employment. However, the Employee shall repay the Employer all amounts paid by the Employer to the Employee under this paragraph that are disallowed, in whole or in part, as deductible to the Employer for income tax purposes.

8. The Employee is also entitled to _____days' paid sick leave for each complete _____ worked for the Employer.
(time period)

However, in order to qualify for any given period of sick leave, the Employee must provide the Employer with a doctor's certificate of the Employee's medical incapacity to work for the period claimed. It is understood and agreed that unused sick leave is lost and will not be compensated for on termination of the Employee's employment with the Employer for any reason.

9. The Employer may terminate the employment of the Employee without cause on _____ weeks' notice to the Employee. However, the Employer reserves the right to terminate the Employee's employment without notice for cause, including but not limited to death, incapacitating illness, incompetence, or failure to follow reasonable employment requests, at any time.

10. The Employee promises to keep the Employer's business secrets confidential during and after the term of employment and the Employee also promises that, on the termination of the Employee's employment with the Employer for any reason, the Employee will not operate a _____ business or in any way aid and assist any other person to operate such a business in _____
(geographical area)

for a period of _____ from the date of termination of the
(time period)

Employee's employment.

11. If any provision or part of any provision in this agreement is void for any reason, it shall be severed without affecting the validity of the balance of the agreement.

12. Except for increases in salary or extension of employment benefits, the terms of this agreement remain in force until amended in writing signed by both parties.

13. There are no representations, warranties, conditions, terms, or collateral contracts affecting the employment contemplated in this agreement except as set out in this agreement.

14. The Employee acknowledges ample opportunity and advice to take independent legal advice in connection with the execution of this employment agreement.

15. This agreement is governed by the laws of the Province/Territory of _____.

Executed under seal on _____.
                                (date)

Signed, sealed, and)
delivered in the presence)
of:)
)
)
_____) _____s
for the Employer) *(Employer signature)*
)
_____) _____s
for the Employee) *(Employee signature)*

EMPLOYEE WARNING NOTICE

_____, 20__

Dear _____:

Re Employment Performance

This is to document our meeting of _____ in which I drew your attention

                                                    (date)

to certain unsatisfactory aspects of your employment performance, namely,

In order to improve your performance, you must:

I will assist you in any reasonable way to meet these requirements.

However, I am giving you fair warning that, if your employment performance does not significantly improve, I will have no option but to terminate your employment for cause.

Yours truly,

_____

(Signature)

Receipt of this warning is acknowledged.

_____   _____

Date   By

SELF-COUNSEL PRESS—Form 403/04

EMPLOYEE DISMISSAL NOTICE

_____, 20__

Dear _____:

Re Termination of Employment

We regret to inform you that your employment with this firm is terminated effective on receipt of this letter for the following reason(s):

Please vacate the premises immediately with your personal possessions.

We will forward your salary earned to date in due course together with any vacation pay to which you are entitled.

Yours truly,

_____
(Signature)

EMPLOYEE COVENANTS

The undersigned Employee (the "Employee") of _____

_____ (the "Employer") hereby promises the Employer:

(name of employer)

1. to keep the Employer's business secrets, including but not limited to customer, supplier, logistical, financial, research, and development information, confidential and not to disclose the Employer's business secrets to any third party during and after the term of the Employee's employment;

GENERAL NON-COMPETITION CLAUSE

2. that, on the termination of the Employee's employment with the Employer for any reason, the Employee will not operate a _____

(type of business)

_____ business or in any way aid and assist any

other person to operate such a business in _____

(geographical area)

for a period of _____ from the date of termination of the Employee's employment;

SPECIFIC ACCOUNT NON-COMPETITION CLAUSE

3. that, on the termination of the Employee's employment with the Employer for any reason, the Employee will not solicit any customer of the Employer that was a customer of the Employer during the course of the Employee's employment with the Employer, whether or not still a customer of the Employer and whether or not knowledge of the customer is considered confidential information, or in any way aid and assist any other person to solicit any such customer for a period of _____

(time period)

from the date of termination of the Employee's employment.

If any part of these promises is void for any reason, the undersigned accepts that it may be severed without affecting the validity or enforceability of the balance of the promises.

Given under seal on _____

(date)

Signed, sealed, and)
delivered in the presence)
of:)
)
)
_____) _____s

for the Employee) *(Employee signature)*

SELF-COUNSEL PRESS—Form 405/04

EMPLOYEE COVENANT: EXPENSE RECOVERY

The undersigned Employee (the "Employee") of _____

_____ (the "Employer") hereby promises the Employer:

      (name of employer)

To repay the Employer all amounts paid by the Employer to the Employee as compensation for or reimbursement of expenses incurred in the course of employment that are disallowed, in whole or in part, as deductible to the Employer for income tax purposes.

Given under seal on _____

                                      (date)

Signed, sealed, and   )
delivered in the presence   )
of:)
)
_____)   _____s
for the Employee   )   *(Employee signature)*

SELF-COUNSEL PRESS—Form 406/04

EMPLOYEE INVENTION COVENANT

The undersigned Employee (the "Employee") of _____

(name of employer)

(the "Employer") hereby promises the Employer:

1. to promptly disclose to the Employer in writing all inventions, discoveries, developments, innovations, and computer programs ("inventions") made, in whole or in part, by the Employee during the course of or in relation to the Employee's employment with the Employer, whether conceived or developed during working hours or not, including but not limited to inventions:

    a) resulting from work performed by the Employee or any other employee of the Employer for the Employer

    b) relating in any manner whatsoever to the present or contemplated business of the Employer, or

    c) resulting from the use of the Employer's time, equipment, materials, or work facilities;

2. to assign and hereby does assign to the Employer all the Employee's interest in and title to inventions required to be disclosed by the Employee to the Employer;

3. to execute at the Employer's request, whether made during or after the Employee's employment with the Employer, any instruments prepared by or on behalf of the Employer or the Employer's successors in title acknowledging or assuring the Employer's interest in and title to inventions required to be disclosed by the Employee to the Employer or assisting the Employer or the Employer's successors in title to obtain any registered copyright, design, patent, or any other industrial property rights whatsoever.

Given under seal on _____

(date)

Signed, sealed, and   )
delivered in the presence   )
of:)
)

_____   )
for the Employee   )   _____

                                                (Employee signature)

5
BUYING

Form 500. Invitation to quote price of goods

An offer to sell must be certain about the subject matter and price at least before it can constitute a legally binding contract. Use this form to obtain a firm price quote.

Fill in the description of the goods you are interested in purchasing in the first line of the body of the letter.

Form 501. Demand for delivery of goods

Use this form to make formal demand for delivery of goods to set up possible repudiation of a purchase order for unreasonable delay in making delivery.

Fill in the description of the goods you ordered in the first line of the body of the letter.

Form 502. Cancellation of purchase order for late delivery

Use this form, with proper legal advice, to formally repudiate a purchase order for delay in making delivery. Note that whether delay in delivery constitutes grounds for repudiating a purchase contract depends on the delivery terms of the contract or, if nothing is said in the contract about the importance of time of delivery, on whether the delay is implicitly unacceptable in the particular circumstance. There may be a lot of room in any particular circumstance for argument about whether the delay is unacceptable.

Fill in the description of the goods you ordered in the first line of the body of the letter.

Send a copy of this letter to your lawyer and fill in name of the lawyer in the last line following "copy to."

Form 503. Rejection of non-conforming goods

Use this form to reject an entire shipment of goods that does not conform to the specifications in your purchase order.

Fill in the specific reasons for the rejection at the end of the first paragraph.

Send a copy to your lawyer and fill in the name of the lawyer in the last line following "copy to."

Form 504. Partial rejection of non-conforming goods

Use this form to reject part of a shipment of goods that does not conform to the specifications in your purchase order.

Fill in specific reasons for rejection of goods at the end of the first paragraph.

Form 505. Request for instruction to return rejected goods

Use this form to request instructions from a would-be vendor on returning rejected goods.

Form 506. Conditional acceptance of non-conforming goods

Use this form where a shipment of goods does not conform to the specifications of a purchase order but you are nonetheless prepared to accept them if the vendor drops its price.

Fill in the specific reasons why the goods do not conform to your specifications at the end of the first paragraph.

Form 507. Election to return goods on approval

Use this form to return goods shipped for examination on approval.

Form 508. Conditional payment for goods reserving rights

Use this form to cover payment for a shipment of goods where you have not had a chance to properly inspect the shipment.

Form 509. Notice of defective goods

Use this form to demand unspecified satisfaction where delivered goods turn out to be defective.

Fill in the specific reasons that the goods are defective at the end of the first paragraph.

Form 510. Stop payment on cheque

Use this form to stop payment on your cheque. Your bank may require a signed specific form of its own. Telephone in the stop payment and follow it up immediately with written confirmation.

INVITATION TO QUOTE PRICE OF GOODS

_____, 20__

Dear _____:

Re Purchase Quote

We are interested in purchasing:

Please quote your ordinary unit price for supplying these goods together with your discount for volume purchases.

Please also indicate:

a) whether your quotes are inclusive or exclusive of sales taxes; if not otherwise stated, we will assume your quotes are inclusive of sales taxes;

b) delivery time from receipt of our purchase order to receipt of your shipment; this time frame will be a condition of any purchase order made;

c) if delivery costs are included in your quotes, your prices for pick-up at our separate cost; if delivery costs are not included in your quotes, please state this clearly; otherwise we will assume they are included;

d) your terms of payment.

All price quotations must be firm and state when they expire.

Yours very truly,

_____

(Signature)

SELF-COUNSEL PRESS—Form 500/04

DEMAND FOR DELIVERY OF GOODS

_____, 20__

Dear _____:

Re Delivery of Purchase Order

We ordered _____

_____

from you on _____ and paid for them by cheque dated
                                    (date)

_____ which has been cashed by you.

We have not yet received delivery of the goods.

Unless we receive immediate delivery of the goods, we shall cancel the order and seek the return of our money, if necessary, by legal action.

Govern yourselves accordingly.

Yours truly,

_____

(Signature)

CANCELLATION OF PURCHASE ORDER FOR LATE DELIVERY

_____, 20__

Dear _____ :

Re Cancellation of Purchase Order

We ordered _____

_____

from you on _____ and paid for them by cheque dated
                        (date)

_____ which has been cashed by you.

We demanded immediate delivery of the goods by letter dated _____.

We still have not received delivery of the goods.

We, therefore, repudiate the order for unreasonable delay in delivery and demand the return of our money.

Please be advised that, unless we receive a refund of our money in this office within 10 days of the date of this letter, we will take legal action to compel the return of our money without further notice to you.

Govern yourselves accordingly.

Yours truly,

_____
(Signature)

copy to:

REJECTION OF NON-CONFORMING GOODS

_____, 20__

Dear _____:

Re Rejection of Delivered Goods

We received a delivery from you further to our purchase order of _____
(date)

but the goods delivered do not conform to the specifications of our order because of:

Accordingly, we reject the shipment and demand the return of our money.

Please be advised that, unless we receive a refund of our money in this office within 10 days of the date of this letter, we will take legal action to compel the return of our money without further notice to you.

Govern yourselves accordingly.

Also please immediately advise us as to the disposition of the rejected goods. We caution you that we will accept no responsibility for their safekeeping if we do not have your instructions as to their disposition within a reasonable time.

Yours truly,

_____
(Signature)

copy to:

PARTIAL REJECTION OF NON-CONFORMING GOODS

_____, 20__

Dear _____:

Re Partial Rejection of Delivered Goods

We received a delivery from you further to our purchase order of _____
(date)

but some of the goods delivered do not conform to the specifications of our order because of:

Accordingly, we reject these goods.

Please immediately arrange for proportionate refund of our purchase order money.

Also please immediately advise us as to the disposition of the rejected goods. We caution you that we will accept no responsibility for their safekeeping if we do not have your instructions as to their disposition within a reasonable time.

Yours truly,

_____
(Signature)

REQUEST FOR INSTRUCTION TO RETURN REJECTED GOODS

_____, 20__

Dear _____:

Re Return of Rejected Goods

Further to the rejection of the goods you delivered in purported fulfillment of our purchase order dated _____, please advise us immediately as to how you wish
        (date)
the goods disposed of.

We caution you that we will accept no responsibility for their safekeeping if we do not have your instructions as to their disposition within a reasonable time.

Yours truly,

_____
(Signature)

CONDITIONAL ACCEPTANCE OF NON-CONFORMING GOODS

_____, 20__

Dear _____:

Re Your Delivery of Non-Conforming Goods

We received a delivery from you further to our purchase order of _____
(date)

but the goods delivered do not conform to the specifications of our order because of:

Although the goods delivered are non-conforming, we are prepared to accept them provided you allow us a credit of $_____ making the total price of our purchase order $_____.

Please contact us immediately with regard to our proposal.

If we do not hear from you within 10 days of the date of this letter, we shall reject the shipment as non-conforming.

Yours very truly,

_____

(Signature)

SELF-COUNSEL PRESS—Form 506/04

ELECTION TO RETURN GOODS ON APPROVAL

_____, 20__

Dear _____:

Re Return of Goods

Please be advised that we are electing to return the accompanying goods received from you on approval.

Yours very truly,

_____

(Signature)

SELF-COUNSEL PRESS—Form 507/04

CONDITIONAL PAYMENT FOR GOODS RESERVING RIGHTS

_____, 20__

Dear _____:

Re Conditional Payment for Goods

We have received a delivery from you further to our purchase order of _____
                                                                         (date)

but have not had an opportunity of making a full and proper inspection of the shipment.

Therefore, we are enclosing payment for the goods expressly reserving our rights with regard to any non-conforming found after full and proper inspection.

Yours very truly,

_____
(Signature)

SELF-COUNSEL PRESS—Form 508/04

NOTICE OF DEFECTIVE GOODS

_____, 20__

Dear _____:

Re Notice of Defective Goods

We received a delivery from you further to our purchase order of _____
                                                                    (date)

but the goods delivered are defective in that they:

Please be advised that unless we receive a satisfactory response from you within 10 days of the date of this letter, we will take legal action to enforce our rights in this unfortunate matter.

Govern yourselves accordingly.

Yours very truly,

_____

(Signature)

copy to:

STOP PAYMENT ON CHEQUE

_____, 20__

Dear _____:

Re Cheque Stop Payment

Further to our telephone instructions of _____
(date)

you are hereby directed to stop payment on presentation of the following cheque:

Account Name:

Account Number:

Cheque Number:

Dated:

Payable to:

Amount:

Please contact the writer for any additional information or explanation required.

Yours very truly,

_____

(Signature)

6
SELLING

Form 600. Bill of sale

At a minimum, a bill of sale provides documentary proof of purchase of goods. Use this form as a template for any basic bill of sale.

Fill in a detailed list of goods following the name of the buyer at the end of the first paragraph.

Form 601. Bill of sale (without warranties)

Use this form to draft a bill of sale excluding vendor warranties. Note that it is signed by the buyer as well as the seller to underline the buyer's acceptance of the terms of sale. Many jurisdictions have "overriding" statutory vendor warranties in consumer sales.

Fill in a detailed list of goods following the name of the buyer at the end of the first paragraph.

Form 602. Bill of sale (with encumbrances)

Use this form to draft a bill of sale subject to encumbrances being assumed by the buyer (e.g., a chattel mortgage). Note that it is an agreement signed by both sides.

Fill in a detailed list of goods following the name of the buyer at the end of the first paragraph.

Fill in the encumbrance description and encumbrance amount at the end of the second paragraph.

Form 603. Receipt for goods

Use this form to obtain the buyer's acknowledgment of receipt of goods in acceptable condition.

Fill in the name of the seller after the "To" at the beginning of the text.

Form 604. Demand for particulars of rejection of goods

Use this form to demand the reason for rejection of a shipment of goods.

Send a copy of this letter to your lawyer and fill in the name of the lawyer in the last line following "copy to."

Form 605. Refusal of rejection of goods

Use this form to reject a buyer's reasons for rejecting a shipment of goods.

Send a copy of this letter to your lawyer and fill in the name of the lawyer in the last line following "copy to."

Form 606. Delivery of substituted goods

Use this form to notify a buyer of delivery of substituted goods where you are unable to fill a purchase order in exact accordance with specifications but are prepared to risk substituting other goods which you think may be acceptable.

Fill in the reasons for your inability to deliver the goods at the end of the first paragraph.

Fill in the explanation of the differences in goods sent and goods ordered at the end of the second paragraph.

Form 607. Rejected goods return instructions

Use this form to instruct a buyer how to return rejected goods. Fill in the description of the goods at the end of the first paragraph. Fill in return instructions at the end of the second paragraph.

Form 608. Replacing rejected goods

Use this form to notify a buyer who has validly rejected goods that you are replacing them.

Fill in the description of rejected goods in the first paragraph.

Fill in the instructions for return at the end of the second paragraph.

Form 609. Inability to fill purchase order

Use this form to notify a buyer that you are unable to fill a purchase order.

Fill in the reason you are unable to fill the purchase order at the end of the first paragraph.

Form 610. Late delivery of goods

Use this form to notify a buyer that delivery of goods will be delayed.

Fill in the reason for the delay at the end of the first paragraph.

Form 611. Liability exclusion clause

Exclusion or limitation clauses attempt to exclude ordinary liability for breach of contract. For obvious reasons, they are frowned on by the courts, and many jurisdictions have simply enacted legislation to override liability in non-consumer sales. Note that the exclusion or limitation is ineffective unless clearly brought to the purchaser's attention at the time of purchase.

Form 612. Limited warranty

Vendor warranties typically limit rather than add to a purchaser's legal rights (e.g., "This warranty is in place of all other warranties") and operate as exclusion clauses. Use this clause, with proper legal advice, to give a limited warranty in consumer sales. Note that the exclusion or limitation, if it can operate at all, is ineffective unless clearly brought to the purchaser's attention at the time of purchase.

BILL OF SALE

For good and valuable consideration (receipt of which is acknowledged), _____

_____ (the "Seller")
(seller's name)

hereby sells and transfers possession of the following goods to _____

_____ (the "Buyer"):
(buyer's name)

The Seller warrants that it owns and has the right to sell the goods to the Buyer and that the goods are sold free and clear of all encumbrances.

Given under seal on _____
(date)

Signed, sealed, and delivered to)
the Buyer in the presence of:)
)
_____)   _____s
Witness   )   *(Seller signature)*

BILL OF SALE (WITHOUT WARRANTIES)

For good and valuable consideration (receipt of which is acknowledged), _____

_____ (the "Seller")

(seller's name)

hereby sells and transfers possession of the following goods in their present condition and location to _____ (the "Buyer"):

(buyer's name)

The Seller warrants that it owns and has the right to sell the goods to the Buyer and that the goods are sold free and clear of all encumbrances but makes no representations and gives no warranties as to merchantability of the goods or as to their fitness for any particular purpose or as to their safe use.

The Buyer acknowledges examining the goods and buying them "as and where is" completely at the Buyer's risk and promises not to make any claims against the Seller based upon alleged express or implied representations, warranties, or collateral agreements as to the merchantability of the goods or as to their fitness for any particular purpose or as to their safe use.

Executed in duplicate under seal on _____

(date)

Signed, sealed, and delivered to   )
the Buyer in the presence of:)
)
_____   )   _____s
Witness   )   Seller

Signed, sealed, and delivered to   )
the Seller in the presence of:)
)
_____   )   _____s
Witness   )   Buyer

BILL OF SALE (WITH ENCUMBRANCES)

For good and valuable consideration (receipt of which is acknowledged), _____
_____ (the "Seller")
(seller's name)

hereby sells and transfers possession of the following goods to _____
_____ (the "Buyer"):
(buyer's name)

The Seller warrants that it owns the goods but stipulates that they are being sold subject to the following encumbrance(s) in the following amount(s):

The Buyer acknowledges buying the goods subject to the above encumbrance(s) and promises to pay the encumbrance(s) and to indemnify and save the Seller harmless from any claim(s) based on failure to pay off the encumbrance(s).

Executed in duplicate under seal on _____
(date)

Signed, sealed, and delivered to   )
the Buyer in the presence of:)
)
_____   ) _____s
Witness   )   Seller

Signed, sealed, and delivered to   )
the Seller in the presence of:)
)
_____   ) _____s
Witness   )   Buyer

RECEIPT FOR GOODS

To:

The undersigned hereby acknowledges receipt of the goods described on the attached purchase or delivery order and that they have been inspected and found without defect in accordance with purchase order specifications.

Dated _____

_____
(Buyer signature)

DEMAND FOR PARTICULARS OF REJECTION OF GOODS

_____, 20__

Dear _____:

Re Rejection of Delivery

We delivered goods to you further to your purchase order of _____
(date)

and you have rejected the shipment without adequate explanation.

Please provide us with the reasons for your rejection of the shipment forthwith.

Unless we get a satisfactory response from you within 10 days of the date of this letter, we will institute legal proceedings against you for the price of the goods without further notice.

Govern yourselves accordingly.

Yours very truly,

_____
(Signature)

copy to:

SELF-COUNSEL PRESS—Form 604/04

REFUSAL OF REJECTION OF GOODS

_____, 20__

Dear _____:

Re Rejection of Delivery

We delivered goods to you further to your purchase order of _____
(date)
and you have rejected the shipment without lawful justification.

Unless we receive payment in full for the goods in this office within 10 days of the date of this letter, we will institute legal proceedings against you for the price of the goods without further notice.

Govern yourselves accordingly.

Yours truly,

_____
(Signature)

copy to:

DELIVERY OF SUBSTITUTED GOODS

_____, 20__

Dear Customer:

Re Notice of Delivery of Substituted Goods

We are in receipt of your purchase order of_____
                                                                                           (date)
but, unfortunately, we are unable to deliver the specific goods you ordered at this time because of:

However, in order to accommodate your apparent needs, we are shipping substituted goods to you which only differ from the specific goods you ordered in that they:

The purchase price of the substituted goods is $_____
If the substituted goods are not acceptable to you, please return them at our expense by the same carrier that delivered them.

We do not expect to have the specific goods you ordered in stock until some time after

_____.
                    (date)

Yours very truly,

_____

(Signature)

SELF-COUNSEL PRESS—Form 606/04

REJECTED GOODS RETURN INSTRUCTIONS

_____, 20__

Dear Customer:

Re Return of Rejected Goods

We acknowledge your rejection of our shipment of:

Please return the shipment to us at our cost by:

We apologize for any inconvenience this may have caused.

Yours very truly,

_____
(Signature)

SELF-COUNSEL PRESS—Form 607/04

REPLACING REJECTED GOODS

_____, 20__

Dear Customer:

Re Notice of Replacing Rejected Goods

We acknowledge your rejection of:

which we shipped to you.

We are immediately shipping replacement goods to you at our cost.

Please return the rejected goods to us also at our cost by:

We apologize for any inconvenience this may have caused.

Yours very truly,

_____

(Signature)

INABILITY TO FILL PURCHASE ORDER

_____, 20__

Dear Customer:

Re Inability to Fill Purchase Order

We have received the attached purchase order but, unfortunately, are unable to fill it because of:

Accordingly, we are returning your order cheque.

We apologize for any inconvenience this may cause.

Yours very truly,

_____
(Signature)

SELF-COUNSEL PRESS—Form 609/04

LATE DELIVERY OF GOODS

_____, 20__

Dear Customer:

Re Notice of Late Delivery

We are in receipt of your purchase order of _____
                                                                            (date)

but, unfortunately, are unable to deliver the goods to you at this time because of:

Please bear with us and we will fulfill your order as soon as we can.

Yours very truly,

_____

(Signature)

LIABILITY EXCLUSION CLAUSE

_____

acknowledges and accepts that_____

is not liable in contract, tort, or equity for any innocent or negligent misrepresentation made in connection with this contract or for any breach of express or implied warranty, condition, or fundamental term of this contract or for any fundamental breach of this contract or for breach of any express or implied duty of care arising in connection with this contract or for any breach of express or implied collateral contract, whether made before, at the same time, or after this contract, touching any matter affected by or affecting this contract.

LIMITED WARRANTY

These goods are warranted free from defects in workmanship and materials on purchase. If the goods are defective, they will be repaired or replaced, at the vendor's option, without charge on return to the vendor within_____

(period of time)

from date of purchase with satisfactory proof of purchase from the vendor and date of purchase.

This warranty is only given to the original purchaser of the goods and is void if the goods have been

_____ damaged by negligence or accident after purchase

_____ used other than for the purpose for which they are intended to be used or not used in accordance with any operating instructions supplied with the goods

_____ adapted or repaired other than by the vendor or an approved service center (if applicable, a list of approved service centers is available from the vendor on request), or

_____ added on to or used with other goods which may affect the integrity, performance, safety, or reliability of these goods.

This warranty is given in place of all other warranties and assurances, whether express or implied, including but not limited to matters of quality, fitness for purpose, or merchantability and the vendor accepts no liability, under any circumstances whatsoever, for any consequential damage or loss suffered by anyone as a result of using or being unable to use the goods.

Certain jurisdictions have consumer protection laws which give you additional rights.

SELF-COUNSEL PRESS—Form 612/04

7
COLLECTIONS

1. SELLER'S FORMS

Form 700. Request for payment

Use this form to request payment of your account.

Form 701. Second request for payment

Use this form to make a second request for payment of your account.

Form 702. Final demand for payment

Use this form to make a final demand for payment of your account prior to instituting collection proceedings.

Form 703. Bad cheque letter

Use this form to notify a payer of a returned cheque.

Form 704. Installment payment agreement

Use this form to document an agreement to pay off a debt with interest in monthly installments.

Form 705. Receipt for payment

Use this form to draft a receipt for payment.

Form 706. Collection instructions to lawyers

Use this form to instruct your lawyer to commence collection proceedings.

Insert a description of the debt in the first paragraph following the full address of the debtor.

Select among the relevant documents by underlining, circling, or highlighting the pertinent ones.

2. BUYER'S FORMS

Form 707. Notice of disputed account

Use this form to notify an alleged creditor that you dispute the creditor's account.

Insert description of account in first paragraph.

Choose the reason for disputing the balance by underlining, circling, or highlighting the correct one.

Form 708. Settlement offer of disputed account

Use this form to make an offer to settle a demand for payment of a disputed account.

Form 709. Agreement to compromise disputed account

Use this form to draft a formal agreement with a vendor to accept a lesser payment on a disputed account.

REQUEST FOR PAYMENT

_____, 20__

Dear _____:

Re Payment of Account

Further to our invoice dated _____ in the amount of $_____,
(date)

we have not yet received payment.

We are sure that this is merely an oversight and would ask you to send the payment now.

Yours very truly,

_____

(Signature)

SELF-COUNSEL PRESS—Form 700/04

SECOND REQUEST FOR PAYMENT

_____, 20__

Dear _____:

Re Second Request for Payment

Further to our invoice dated _____in the amount of $ _____,
(date)

and our request for payment of _____, we still have not received
(date)

payment.

Again we would ask you to send the payment now.

Yours very truly,

_____

(Signature)

SELF-COUNSEL PRESS—Form 701/04

FINAL DEMAND FOR PAYMENT

_____, 20__

Dear_____:

Re Final Demand for Payment

Further to our invoice dated _____ in the amount of $ _____,
(date)

we have not yet received payment.

Please be advised that unless we receive payment in full of our invoice in this office within 10 days of the date of this letter, we will institute collection proceedings without further notice to you.

These proceedings will include claims for pre-judgment interest and legal costs and will substantially increase the amount owing by you to us.

Govern yourselves accordingly.

Yours very truly,

_____

(Signature)

SELF-COUNSEL PRESS—Form 702/04

BAD CHEQUE LETTER

_____, 20__

Dear _____:

Re Bad Cheque

Please be advised that your cheque to us dated _____ has been returned because of insufficient funds.

This is a serious matter, and we would ask you to replace the cheque immediately.

Unless we have a replacement cheque in this office within 10 days of the date of this letter, we will institute collection proceedings without further notice to you.

These proceedings will include claims for pre-judgment interest and legal costs and will substantially increase the amount owing by you to us.

Govern yourselves accordingly.

Yours very truly,

_____

(Signature)

INSTALLMENT PAYMENT AGREEMENT

_____, 20__

Dear _____:

Re Installment Payment Arrangement

This is to confirm the arrangement under which we will accept payment of our outstanding account of $_____in installments.

You will sign and return the enclosed copy of this letter indicating admission of the full amount of the account and acceptance of the terms of our agreement.

We will, then, accept payment of the account, together with interest at the rate of _____% per annum, calculated semi-annually not in advance, in consecutive, monthly installments of $_____, commencing_____ and continuing on the
(date)

_____of each successive month until paid off in full. Time will be considered to be of
(day)

the essence of this arrangement. Each payment will be applied, first, to accrued interest and, second, to principal.

If there is default in making any payment, at our option the full balance owing on the account, together with accrued agreed interest, shall immediately become due and payable and continue to accrue interest, before and after judgment at the same rate of interest until paid off in full.

Please return the signed copy of this agreement with your first payment before the commencement date of the monthly installments; otherwise this agreement is null and void.

Yours very truly,

_____

(Signature)

Admission and Acceptance

The undersigned hereby admits the full amount of the above outstanding account and having no rights of set-off or counterclaim and accepts the above terms of payment.

Dated _____20____   _____
                                                             (Signature)

RECEIPT FOR PAYMENT

_____ 20___

RECEIVED FROM _____

_____DOLLARS

$_____ FOR _____

_____

_____
(Signature)

COLLECTION INSTRUCTIONS TO LAWYERS

_____, 20__

Dear _____ :

Re Institution of Collection Proceedings

Please accept this letter as your instructions to immediately commence collection proceedings on our behalf against _____
(full name of debtor)

of _____
(full address of debtor)

for _____
(describe debt)

in the amount of \$_____ .

We enclose copies of the relevant documents:

_____ purchase order

_____ invoice

_____ bad cheque and notice of return

_____ correspondence

for your file. We shall keep the original documents safe for production in court as necessary.

If you need further documents or information, please contact the writer.

Please include claims for pre-judgment interest and legal costs with the claim for the amount of the invoice.

We would ask you to keep us informed of the progress of this matter and to consult us when our legal bill reaches \$_____ .

Yours very truly,

_____
(Signature)
Encs.

NOTICE OF DISPUTED ACCOUNT

_____, 20__

Dear _____:

Re Disputed Account

We acknowledge receipt of your statement of account for _____

_____

(describe)

dated _____.

We dispute:

Please contact the writer immediately to discuss the adjustment of our account.

Yours very truly,

_____

(Signature)

SETTLEMENT OFFER OF DISPUTED ACCOUNT

_____, 20__

Dear _____:

Re Disputed Account

This is in connection with the demand for payment of your invoice dated _____.

As you know, we dispute the balance indicated as owing by us.

Without admitting liability and solely for the purpose of a quick resolution of this unfortunate matter, we are prepared to offer an immediate payment of $_____ in full settlement of your disputed account.

If this proposal is acceptable to you, please advise us in writing and we will send the payment by return mail.

Yours very truly,

_____
(Signature)

SELF-COUNSEL PRESS—Form 708/04

AGREEMENT TO COMPROMISE DISPUTED ACCOUNT

Whereas _____
(claimant's name)

(the "Claimant") has a claim against _____
(disputant's name)

(the "Disputant") on a disputed invoice dated _____ in the amount of $_____.

It is agreed as follows:

1. The Claimant will accept a lesser payment of $_____ in full settlement of its claim on the invoice.

2. If the Disputant does not pay the lesser payment in full to the Claimant within _____ days of receipt back of an original copy of this agreement executed by both parties, the Claimant may sue the Disputant for the full amount of its disputed invoice.

3. If the Claimant's claim on its disputed invoice is compromised pursuant to this agreement, the parties mutually release each other from any and all claims and rights of action against each other, present and future, arising in connection with their dispute over payment of the disputed invoice.

4. This agreement binds and benefits the parties and their respective heirs, executors, administrators, personal representatives, successors, and assigns.

Executed in duplicate under seal on_____.
(date)

Signed, sealed, and delivered in the presence of:	)	
	)	
	)	
	)	
_____	)	_____s
for the Disputant	)	The Disputant
	)	
_____	)	_____s
for the Claimant	)	The Claimant

SELF-COUNSEL PRESS—Form 709/04

8
CREDIT/DEBIT

Form 800. Personal credit application

Use this form to obtain credit information. Be careful about disclosing credit information obtained from a customer to third parties the information was probably given in confidence and there may be laws regulating its disclosure.

Insert name of your firm at the end of the section titled, "Certificate."

Form 801. Authority to release credit information

Use this form to obtain the customer's authority to disclose and release credit information from a specific source to your firm. The disclosure of credit-related information about a customer may be regulated by law.

Form 802. Demand promissory note

Promissory notes are special promises to pay which can be endorsed over to someone else like cheques. They are frequently used as simple documentary evidence of indebtedness. Use this form to draw up a simple promissory note payable on demand.

Form 803. Joint and several demand promissory note

Use this form to draw up a simple promissory note payable by more than one person on demand.

Form 804. Due date promissory note

Use this form to draw up a simple promissory note payable on a specified future date.

Form 805. Series form promissory note

Use this form to draw up a series of installment payment promissory notes.

Form 806. Periodic payment promissory note

Use this form to draw up a single promissory note providing for installment payments.

Form 807. Demand for payment on demand promissory note

A demand promissory note requires a demand for payment to make it due and payable. Use this form to make demand for payment on a demand promissory note. Note that "payable on demand" means "payable within a reasonably prompt time after demand," which depends on the circumstances.

Form 808. Payment in full demand on installment promissory note

Use this form to make demand for accelerated payment in full of an installment promissory note which provides for the whole balance becoming due on default in making an installment payment.

Send a copy of this letter to your lawyer. Insert your lawyer's name following "copy to."

Form 809. Installment payment demand on promissory note

Use this form to make demand for payment of an overdue installment under an installment promissory note which provides for the whole balance becoming due on default in making an installment payment. The next step is demanding payment of the whole balance.

Form 810. Guarantee

Use this form to draft a guarantee of payment by a third party.

Form 811. Demand for payment on guarantee

Use this form to demand payment on a guarantee.

Send a copy of this letter to your lawyer. Insert your lawyer's name following "copy to."

PERSONAL CREDIT APPLICATION

Full name of applicant:_____

Present address:_____

_____

Home phone: (   )_____Work phone: (   )_____

HOME:

Do you rent or own your present address? (   ) rent (   ) own

How many years have you lived at your present address?

Previous address(es):

_____

from _____to_____

_____

from _____to_____

_____

from _____to_____

WORK:

Are you employed or in business? (   ) employed (   ) in business

IF EMPLOYED:

What is your present employment? _____

Name of your present employer? _____

Present employer's address? _____

_____

How many years have you worked for your present employer? _____

IF IN BUSINESS:

What type of business are you in? _____

Name of business? _____

Address of business? _____

_____

How many years have you owned this business? _____

SELF-COUNSEL PRESS—Form 800/04

IF EMPLOYED OR OWNED BUSINESS LESS THAN TWO YEARS:

Previous employment_____

Name of previous employer _____

Previous employer's address _____

_____

How many years did you work for your previous employer?_____

ANNUAL INCOME:

Gross base income from employment	$_____
Gross overtime income	$_____
Gross income from commissions	$_____
Net income from business	$_____
Net rental income	$_____
Dividend/interest income	$_____
Other income (specify):	$_____
	$_____
Total annual income	$_____

ASSETS (estimate value):		DEBTS (estimate amount):	
Home	$_____	Mortgage	$_____
Car	$_____	Car loan	$_____
Savings/Bonds	$_____	Bank loan	$_____
	$_____	Credit cards	$_____
	$_____		$_____
	$_____		$_____
	$_____		$_____
	$_____		$_____
	$_____		$_____
Total assets	$_____	Total debts:	$_____

BANKRUPTCY: Have you gone bankrupt in the last five years? (   ) yes (   ) no

If yes, give date of assignment: _____

CERTIFICATE: I certify the above information to be accurate and complete and hereby authorize the disclosure and release of any credit-related information about myself to

_____
(firm name)

Dated:_____   Signed:_____

AUTHORITY TO RELEASE CREDIT INFORMATION

To: _____

(information holder)

From: _____

(credit applicant)

The undersigned hereby authorizes the disclosure and release of any and all personal credit-related information in your possession, including but not limited to credit, financial, salary, banking, debt, and tax information and materials, to _____

_____

(your firm name)

as required, until further notice.

Dated _____

Witness _____   Credit Applicant _____

DEMAND PROMISSORY NOTE

$_____

For value received, the undersigned promises to pay _____

(payee)

or order on demand the sum of _____

dollars, together with interest from this date at the rate of _____ % per annum, both before and after default, until paid in full.

Signed at _____ on _____

_____   _____
Witness   Promissor

SELF-COUNSEL PRESS—Form 802/04

JOINT AND SEVERAL DEMAND PROMISSORY NOTE

$_____

For value received, the undersigned, jointly and severally promise to pay_____
                                                                                    (payee)

or order on demand the sum of _____dollars, together with interest

from this date at the rate of _____% per annum, both before and after default,

until paid in full.

Signed at _____   on _____

_____   _____
Witness   Promissor 1

_____   _____
Witness   Promissor 2

SELF-COUNSEL PRESS—Form 803/04

DUE DATE PROMISSORY NOTE

$_____

For value received, the undersigned promises to pay _____
(payee)

or order on or before _____ the sum of _____
(date)

dollars, together with interest from this date at the rate _____% per annum

both before and after default, until paid in full.

Signed at _____ on _____

_____   _____
Witness   Promissor

SELF-COUNSEL PRESS—Form 804/04

SERIES FORM PROMISSORY NOTE

$_____

For value received, the undersigned promises to pay _____
(payee)

or order on or before _____ the sum of _____
(date)

dollars, together with interest from this date at the rate of _____% per annum, both before and after default, until paid in full.

This note is No._____ in a series of _____ notes given by

_____
(debtor)

to secure payment of a principal debt in the total amount of _____ dollars ($_____).

If there is a default in the payment of this note, at the option of its holder, any remaining notes in the series also held by the holder, shall immediately become due and payable.

Signed at _____   on _____

_____   _____
Witness   Promissor

SELF-COUNSEL PRESS—Form 805/04

PERIODIC PAYMENT PROMISSORY NOTE

$_____

For value received, the undersigned promises to pay _____
(payee)

or order the principal sum of _____ dollars, together with interest
from this date at the rate of _____% per annum, both before and after default,
until paid in full, in monthly installments of _____ dollars
($ _____), commencing _____ and on the
_____ day of each successive month, until _____ when
any unpaid principal and accrued interest on the note shall become due and payable.

This note may be prepaid in whole or in part at any time without penalty.

All payments on this note shall be made at _____

_____
(address)

during normal business hours or at such other reasonable place as the holder may designate in
writing from time to time.

All payments and prepayments made on this note shall be applied first to accrued interest and
then to principal.

If there is a default in making the monthly payments on this note, at the option of its holder, its
unpaid principal and accrued interest shall immediately become due and payable.

For value received, if there is a default in making any payment on this note, the undersigned also
promises to pay _____
(payee)

on demand all reasonably incurred costs of enforcing payment on the note, including but not
necessarily limited to, legal costs.

The undersigned waives presentation for payment, notice of non-payment, protest, and notice of
protest in connection with this note.

Signed at _____   on _____

_____   _____
Witness   Promissor

DEMAND FOR PAYMENT ON DEMAND PROMISSORY NOTE

_____, 20__

Dear _____:

Re Demand for Payment on Note

I am the holder of your promissory note dated _____ in the amount of $_____, payable to _____
(payee)

or order on demand.

I am making formal demand for payment by you at _____
_____
(address)

of the full, unpaid balance of the note, together with all accrued and accruing interest, within a reasonable time of receipt of this letter.

Please be advised that a reasonable time for payment on a demand note is relatively short.

Yours truly,

_____
(Signature)

PAYMENT IN FULL DEMAND ON INSTALLMENT PROMISSORY NOTE

_____, 20__

Dear _____:

Re Demand for Payment on Note

I am the holder of your promissory note dated _____ in the amount of $_____
payable to _____ or order.
                    (payee)

You are in default on the note for failure to pay the installment due on _____
                                 (date)

in the amount of $_____.

I am, therefore, demanding immediate payment of the full, unpaid balance of the note together with all accrued and accruing interest.

Unless I receive payment of the note in full in this office within 10 days of the date of this letter, I will take legal action to enforce payment without further notice to you.

Govern yourself accordingly.

Yours truly,

_____

(Signature)

copy to:

INSTALLMENT PAYMENT DEMAND ON PROMISSORY NOTE

_____, 20__

Dear _____:

Re Demand for Installment Payment on Note

I am the holder of your installment promissory note dated _____
in the amount of $_____ payable to_____
                                                          (payee)
or order.

You are in default on the note for failure to pay the installment due on _____
                                                                          (date)
in the amount of $_____.

Unless I receive payment of the installment in full in this office within 10 days of the date of this letter, I will demand immediate payment of the remaining balance of the note.

Govern yourself accordingly.

Yours truly,

_____
(Signature)

SELF-COUNSEL PRESS—Form 809/04

GUARANTEE

In consideration of _____

(the "Creditor")

accepting the payment promise of _____

(the "Debtor")

the undersigned _____

(the "Guarantor")

hereby unconditionally guarantees the Creditor prompt and full payment of all amounts which are now or may become owing by the Debtor to the Creditor.

The obligation of the Guarantor under this guarantee is limited to a maximum amount of _____dollars ($_____).

This guarantee is intended to operate notwithstanding any renewals, extensions, or indulgences of any kind granted the Debtor by the Creditor, or the release or change of any security given by the Debtor to the Creditor to secure the Debtor's payment promise ("Security"), or any failure or neglect on the part of the Creditor to enforce payment by the Debtor or to protect any Security, and the Creditor may call upon the guarantee as a first principal obligation without previously demanding payment from the Debtor or any co-guarantor or realizing any Security.

This guarantee is also intended to operate as a continuing, absolute obligation and remains in force until revoked by notice in writing from the Guarantor to the Creditor, which revocation shall not affect the guarantee of prompt and full payment of any amount owed by the Debtor to the Creditor as of the date of actual receipt of notice of revocation by the Creditor.

If more than one person executes this guarantee, their obligation under this guarantee is joint and several.

Given under seal on _____.

(date)

Signed, sealed, and   )
delivered in the presence   )
of:)
)
_____   )   _____ s
for   )
)
_____   )   _____ s
for   )

SELF-COUNSEL PRESS—Form 810/04

DEMAND FOR PAYMENT ON GUARANTEE

_____, 20__

Dear _____:

Re Demand for Payment on Guarantee

We hold your guarantee dated _____ for the indebtedness to us of
_____
(Debtor)

This is to advise you that the indebtedness has reached the amount of $_____, including interest, as set out in the enclosed statement of account.

Please be advised that unless we receive payment of the indebtedness in this office within 10 days of the date of this letter, we will institute collection proceedings against the debtor and you without further notice.

These proceedings will include claims for pre-judgment interest and legal costs and will substantially increase the amount owing by you to us.

Govern yourself accordingly.

Yours truly,

_____
(Signature)

copy to:

9
LEASES

Form 900. Commercial lease

Use this form with proper legal advice, to draft a lease of commercial premises. Do not use this form for residential premises because many jurisdictions have special legislation governing and protecting residential tenancies.

In section 4(b), for "additional rent," insert items such as landlord's business taxes, property taxes, school taxes, repairs to building, heating, water rates, electric rates, maintenance costs, building security, management fees, and landlord's fire and public liability insurance premiums.

In section 5, insert as sole responsibility and expense of the Tenant items such as tenant's business taxes, repairs to premises, utilities separately metered, leasehold improvements, and janitorial services.

In section 6, insert as sole responsibility and expense of the landlord items such as landlord's business taxes, property taxes, school taxes, repairs to building, heating, water rates, electric rates, maintenance costs, building security, management fees, and landlord's fire and public liability insurance premiums.

Form 901. Exercising option to renew lease

Use this form to exercise an option to renew a lease.

Form 902. Notice of rent default

Use this form to demand payment of arrears of rent under a commercial lease.

Form 903. Notice of other lease default

Use this form to demand remedy of default under a commercial lease other than in connection with payment of rent.

Insert specifics of breach of lease at end of first paragraph.

Form 904. Landlord notice of termination of lease

Use this form to give landlord's notice of terminating a commercial lease. Note that this is appropriate both on expiration of a fixed lease term to prevent the tenant overholding "with consent" and, with proper legal advice, to terminate an informal, periodic (e.g., month-to-month) lease.

Form 905. Tenant notice of termination of lease

Use this form to give tenant's notice of quitting a commercial lease.

Form 906. Agreement to cancel lease

Use this form to draft an agreement to cancel a lease.

Form 907. Assignment of lease

Use this form to draft an assignment of lease. Note the involvement of the landlord in the assignment because most leases are expressed to be non-assignable without the landlord's consent.

Form 908. Amendment of lease

Use this form, preferably with proper legal advice, to draft commercial lease amendments.

Insert particulars of amendment at the end of the third paragraph following "as follows."

Form 909. Commercial sublease

Use this form, preferably with proper legal advice, to draft a sublease of commercial premises.

COMMERCIAL LEASE

This lease is made in duplicate between:

(1)_____ (the "Landlord")

(landlord name)

and

(2)_____ (the "Tenant")

(tenant name)

The Landlord and the Tenant hereby agree as follows:

1.   The Landlord hereby grants the Tenant a lease of the premises outlined in red on the floor plan attached as Schedule A located on the_____

(number)

floor of_____

(address)

_____ (the "Premises").

The parties agree that the Premises have a rented area of _____square feet, excluding the exterior walls.

2.   The term of this lease commences on _____ and
ends on _____. If the Tenant continues in occupation of the Premises with the consent of the Landlord after expiry of the term of this lease, the Tenant shall be deemed to be leasing the Premises on a month-to-month basis but otherwise on the same terms as set out in this lease.

3.   The Tenant may use the Premises for_____

(business purpose)

and for no other purpose.

4.   (a) The Tenant shall pay the Landlord a "base rent" of _____dollars ($_____) per year in equal monthly instalments of _____ dollars ($ _____) in advance on or before the first of each month commencing on _____with the base rent for any broken portion of a calendar month in which this lease terminates being prorated.

(b) The following services and expenses are the responsibility of the Landlord, _____% of the total cost of which services and expenses during the term of this lease shall be paid by the Tenant to the Landlord as "additional rent":

(c) The Landlord shall invoice the Tenant monthly for additional rent incurred during the preceding calendar month. Each invoice is payable in full thirty days after delivery. The Tenant is deemed to have admitted the accuracy of the amount charged in any invoice for additional rent which he or she has not challenged in writing within the same thirty days.

(d) The Tenant shall also pay the Landlord as "additional rent", on demand, 100% of the total costs reasonably incurred by the Landlord, including but not limited to legal fees, of curing any default of the Tenant under this lease, including but not limited to enforcing payment of rent and regaining lawful possession of the Premises.

5.   The following services and expenses are the sole responsibility and expense of the Tenant:

6.   The following services and expenses are the sole responsibility and expense of the Landlord:

7.   The Landlord shall also be solely responsible for repairs or improvements to the structure and to the exterior of the building.

8.   Any services and expenses relevant to the use by the Tenant of the Premises and not mentioned in this lease are the responsibility and expense of the Tenant.

9.   The Landlord covenants with the Tenant that so long as the Tenant complies with the terms of this lease, the Tenant may occupy and enjoy the Premises without any interruption from the Landlord.

10.   The Landlord is not liable for any damage to the Tenant's property or for any injury to any person in or coming to or from the Premises, however caused, and the Tenant agrees to indemnify the Landlord against the financial consequences of any such liability. In this regard, the Tenant shall purchase and maintain public liability insurance in the amount of no less than _____dollars ($ _____) and shall provide proof of this insurance to the Landlord on request.

11. The Landlord may terminate this lease for any one of the following or any other cause permitted by law:

  (a) fifteen days' arrears of rent or additional rent;

  (b) the bankruptcy or insolvency of the Tenant;

  (c) a material change in the use of the Premises by the Tenant, and in particular (without limiting the generality of this provision) any change which affects the Landlord's building insurance or which constitutes a nuisance.

  (d) any unauthorized assignment or subletting of this lease by the Tenant;

  (e) substantial damage to or destruction of the Premises;

  (f) any sale or material change in use of the building in which the Premises are located by the Landlord;

  (g) any significant wilful or negligent damage to the Premises caused by the Tenant or by persons permitted on the Premises by the Tenant.

12. The Tenant may not assign or sublet the Premises, in whole or in part, or allow the Premises to be used by any other person without the written consent of the Landlord, which consent may not be unreasonably withheld.

13. The Tenant shall keep the Premises in a reasonable state of repair and cleanliness and shall not make improvements or alterations to the Premises without the written consent of the Landlord, which consent shall not be unreasonably withheld.

14. At the end of the lease, the Tenant shall deliver vacant possession to the Landlord of the Premises in the same condition as at the commencement of the lease, reasonable wear and tear excepted and except that the Landlord may, in the Landlord's sole discretion, elect to keep any of the Tenant's improvements, alterations, or fixtures.

15. Any written notice required or permitted to be given by this lease is sufficiently given if sent in proper form by ordinary mail to the last known address of the party for whom the notice is intended. Any written notice sent by ordinary mail in accordance with this paragraph is deemed, for the purposes of this lease, received by the addressee on the seventh day after mailing unless actually received before. Nothing in this paragraph prevents giving written notice in any other manner recognized by law.

16. In this lease, words importing the singular include the plural, and vice versa, and importing the masculine gender include the feminine, and importing an individual include a corporation and vice versa. This lease binds and benefits the parties and their respective heirs, successors, and permitted assigns.

SELF-COUNSEL PRESS—Form 900/04

17.   If not in default under this lease, the Tenant has the right to renew this lease for a further term of _____ years exercisable by giving written notice of renewal to the Landlord in the six-month period immediately before the expiry of the original fixed term of this lease. The renewed lease is granted on the same terms as set out in this lease except as to base rent and without any further right of renewal. The base rent payable by the Tenant in the renewed term may be agreed between the Landlord and Tenant but, failing such agreement before commencement of the renewed term of the lease, the amount of the base rent shall be referred to and settled by a single arbitrator agreed upon by the parties or, in default of such agreement, to a single arbitrator appointed pursuant to the legislation governing submissions to arbitration in the jurisdiction whose laws govern this agreement. The decision of the arbitrator is final and binding on the parties with no right of appeal.

Executed under seal on_____ .
                                           (date)

Signed, sealed, and   )
delivered in the presence   )
of:)
)
_____   )   _____s
for the Landlord   )   The Landlord
)
_____   )   _____s
for the Tenant   )   The Tenant

EXERCISING OPTION TO RENEW LEASE

_____, 20__

Dear _____:

Re Renewal of lease

This is to notify you that we are exercising the option to renew our lease of_____
_____
(address)

for a further term of _____years contained in _____
(section reference)

of the lease.

— IF ARBITRATED RENT

Please advise us of the rent you propose to charge in the renewed term so that we can decide whether or not to submit the matter to arbitration in accordance with the provisions of _____
_____of the lease.
(section reference)

Yours very truly,

_____
(Signature)

NOTICE OF RENT DEFAULT

_____, 20__

Dear _____:

Re Rent Arrears

You are presently in arrears of rent in the amount of $_____in connection
with your lease of _____.
(address)

Please remedy this situation within 10 days of the date of this letter or we will terminate the lease
and institute collection proceedings without further notice to you.

Yours truly,

_____

(Signature)

NOTICE OF OTHER LEASE DEFAULT

_____, 20__

Dear _____:

Re Lease Default

You are presently in breach of _____ of your lease of _____
                               (section reference)

_____
                                    (address)

by reason of _____

_____

_____

_____

_____

Please remedy this situation within a reasonable time or we will terminate the lease.

Yours truly,

_____

(Signature)

SELF-COUNSEL PRESS—Form 903/04

LANDLORD NOTICE OF TERMINATION OF LEASE

_____, 20__

Dear _____:

Re Notice of Termination of Lease

This is to notify you to quit and deliver up possession of _____
_____
(address)

you presently occupy as our tenant, by_____.
(date)

We remind you of your obligation to leave the premises in a reasonable condition at the end of your tenancy.

Yours truly,

_____
(Signature)

SELF-COUNSEL PRESS—Form 904/04

TENANT NOTICE OF TERMINATION OF LEASE

_____, 20__

Dear _____:

Re Notice of Termination of Lease

This is to notify you of our intention to quit and deliver up possession of _____
_____
(address)
which we presently occupy as your tenant, on _____
(date)

Yours truly,

_____
(Signature)

AGREEMENT TO CANCEL LEASE

Whereas

_____(the "Landlord")

(landlord name)

and

_____(the "Tenant")

(tenant name)

executed a lease dated _____(the "Lease") of certain premises located at

_____(the "Premises")

(address)

but the parties now wish to cancel the Lease;

It is agreed as follows:

    1. In return for the Tenant vacating the Premises on or before _____,

(the "Termination Date")

the Lease is cancelled effective that date and the parties will have no further obligation to each other under the Lease.

    2. Nothing in this agreement operates to discharge obligations and liabilities accrued under the Lease up to the date of its cancellation.

    3. If the Tenant does not vacate the Premises on or before the Termination Date, this agreement is null and void.

    4. This agreement binds and benefits the parties and their respective heirs, executors, administrators, personal representatives, successors, and assigns.

Executed in duplicate under seal on _____.

(date)

Signed, sealed, and delivered in the presence of:	)	
	)	
	)	
	)	
_____)		_____s
for the Landlord	)	The Landlord
	)	
_____)		_____s
for the Tenant	)	The Tenant

ASSIGNMENT OF LEASE

Whereas

_____ (the "Landlord")

(landlord name)

and

_____ (the "Present Tenant")

(present tenant name)

have entered into the lease appended as Schedule A to this assignment (the "Lease"); And whereas the Present Tenant wishes to assign its rights and interest in the Lease to _____ _____the "Proposed Tenant" and the Landlord consents to the assignment;

(proposed tenant name)

It is agreed as follows:

1. The Present Tenant hereby assigns all its rights and interest in the Lease to the Proposed Tenant.

2. The Landlord hereby consents to the assignment.

3. The Proposed Tenant covenants with the Landlord and the Present Tenant to observe and perform all the terms of the Lease.

— TO RELEASE PRESENT TENANT'S LIABILITY

4. The Landlord hereby releases the Present Tenant from all further liability under the Lease but nothing in this assignment operates to discharge obligations and liabilities accrued under the Lease up to the date of this assignment.

[OR]

— TO RETAIN PRESENT TENANT'S LIABILITY

4. Nothing in this assignment operates to release the Present Tenant from its obligations and liabilities under the Lease.

SELF-COUNSEL PRESS—Form 907/04

5. This assignment binds and benefits the parties and their respective heirs, executors, administrators, personal representatives, successors and assigns.

Executed in duplicate under seal on _____.
(date)

Signed, sealed, and delivered in the presence of:	)	
	)	
	)	
	)	
_____	)	_____s
for the Present Tenant	)	The Present Tenant
	)	
_____	)	_____s
for the Proposed Tenant	)	The Proposed Tenant
	)	
_____	)	_____s
for the Landlord	)	The Landlord

AMENDMENT OF LEASE

Whereas

_____(the "Landlord")
(landlord name)

and

_____(the "Tenant")
(tenant name)

have entered into the lease of which a copy is appended as Schedule A to this agreement (the "Lease");

And whereas the Landlord and the Tenant wish to amend the terms of the Lease;

The parties agree to amend the Lease as follows:

All other terms of the Lease remain as stated.

Executed in duplicate under seal on _____.
(date)

Signed, sealed, and   )
delivered in the presence   )
of:)
)
_____   )   _____ s
for the Tenant   )   The Tenant
)
_____   )   _____ s
for the Landlord   )   The Landlord

SELF-COUNSEL PRESS—Form 908/04

COMMERCIAL SUBLEASE

This sublease is made between:

(1) _____(the "Sublandlord")
(sublandlord name)

and

(2) _____(the "Subtenant").
(subtenant name)

Whereas

_____ (the "Landlord")
(landlord name)

and the Sublandlord have entered into a lease of premises (the "Premises") of which a copy is appended as Schedule A to this agreement (the "Lease");

And whereas the Sublandlord and the Subtenant wish to enter into a sublease of the Premises for the balance of the term of the Lease less one day;

And whereas the Landlord has consented to this sublease;

The Sublandlord and Subtenant agree as follows:

1. The Sublandlord hereby subleases the Premises to the Subtenant to have and to hold for the balance of the term of the Lease less one day commencing on _____.

The Subtenant, however, may not assign or sublease its interest in the Premises without the consent of the Sublandlord, which consent expressly may be unreasonably withheld.

2. The Subtenant shall pay rent of _____ dollars ($ _____) per month in advance on the first day of each and every month during the term of this sublease with the rent for any broken portion of a calendar month in which this sublease terminates being prorated.

3. The Subtenant agrees to pay to the Sublandlord all sums which the Sublandlord is required to pay to the Landlord under the Lease as additional rent pursuant to the provisions of the Lease or is required to pay to the Landlord by reason of the Subtenant's occupancy of the Premises.

4. The Subtenant agrees to observe and perform all the Sublandlord's covenants in the Lease apart from the payment of rent and additional rent to the Landlord.

5. The Subtenant shall pay all business taxes in respect of the business carried on by the Subtenant in and upon or by reason of its occupancy of the Premises.

6. The Subtenant shall take out and keep in force during the term of the sublease such insurance in respect of the Premises as to comply with the obligations of the Sublandlord under the Lease and shall be subject, as regards both the Landlord and the Sublandlord, to the same obligations and same limitations of liability with respect to damage, loss, or injury as are set out in the Lease between the Landlord and the Sublandlord.

7. The Sublandlord covenants with the Subtenant:

a)   for quiet enjoyment of the Premises;

b)   to pay all rent and additional rent reserved under the Lease;

c)   to enforce for the benefit of the Subtenant of the Premises the obligations of the Landlord under the Lease with the intent that the benefit of such covenants extend to the Premises to be enjoyed by the Subtenant; the Subtenant, however, agrees to pay the Sublandlord's costs, including but not limited to legal costs, reasonably incurred by the Sublandlord in relation to such enforcement.

8. The rights and obligations of the Subtenant with respect to the installation, alteration or removal of fixtures and improvements and signs shall be governed by the applicable provisions of the Lease.

9. The provisions of the Lease regarding the Landlord's remedies against the Sublandlord and the Premises in connection with the Sublandlord's default under the Lease are hereby incorporated in this sublease for the benefit of the Sublandlord against the Subtenant and the Premises in connection with the Subtenant's default under this sublease.

Executed in duplicate under seal on _____.
                                                      (date)

Signed, sealed, and   )
delivered in the presence   )
of:)
)
_____   )   _____ s
for the Sublandlord   )   The Sublandlord
)
_____   )   _____ s
for the Subtenant   )   The Subtenant

10
ASSIGNMENTS

Form 1000. Assignment with warranties

Use this form for the general set-up of a simple assignment with warranties. An assignment is used for the transfer of the benefit of legal rights (e.g., the benefit of a contract). Note that the Assignor should also give the person owing the obligation involved in the legal right notice of the assignment in order to ensure the person directs the subsequent benefit of the legal right to the Assignee. Remember there must be a right to make the assignment in order for the assignment to work. For example, in lease situations, the landlord often restricts the right to assign the lease without the landlord's consent.

Insert the description of subject matter of assignment in the first paragraph in the proper space.

Form 1001. Assignment without warranties

Use this form for the general set-up of a simple assignment without warranties.

Insert the description of subject matter of assignment in the first paragraph in the proper space.

Form 1002. Assignment of money due

Use this form to assign money due under a simple statement of account. Note provisions for optional acknowledgment of notice of the assignment by the person owing the money.

Form 1003. Assignment of real estate contract

Use this form to assign the purchaser's benefit of an agreement of purchase and sale of real property.

Insert description of property in the first paragraph in the proper space.

Form 1004. Assignment of contract

Use this form, with proper legal advice, to assign the general benefit of a contract (e.g., a car lease).

Form 1005. Assignment of copyright

Use this form to assign the copyright in some original writing. Notice of the assignment is not necessary where the "author" of the writing is the Assignor.

Insert description of writing in first paragraph before "(the "Work")."

Form 1006. Notice of assignment

Use this form to give notice of an assignment to the person under the legal obligation in connection with the assigned contract/debt.

Insert description of subject matter of assignment in first paragraph in the proper space.

Form 1007. Cheque endorsements

Use these examples to draft cheque endorsements which, in effect, assign the payment benefit of a cheque. Write what is indicated on the back of the cheque. Each signature is, of course, the signature of the person to whom the cheque is originally made out to the Payee. The person receiving the endorsed cheque can re-endorse it over to someone else.

Note that you cannot endorse a cheque that is payable only to a named person.

ASSIGNMENT WITH WARRANTIES

For value received, which is acknowledged, _____
(assignor name)

(the "Assignor") hereby assigns all interest owned in _____

_____

to_____ (the "Assignee").
(assignee name)

The Assignor also warrants to the Assignee that the Assignor owns the subject matter of this assignment and has the right to make this assignment without the consent of any third party.

Given under seal on _____.
(date)

Signed, sealed, and   )
delivered in the presence   )
of:)
)
_____   )   _____s
for the Assignor   )   The Assignor

ASSIGNMENT WITHOUT WARRANTIES

For value received, which is acknowledged, _____
(assignor name)

_____(the "Assignor") hereby assigns all interest owned in _____

to_____ (the "Assignee").
(assignee name)

The Assignor stipulates, however, that this assignment is made completely at the risk of the Assignee without any representations, warranties, or collateral assurances of any kind whatsoever with regard to the subject matter of this assignment, its ownership, or the right to make this assignment.

Given under seal on _____.
(date)

Signed, sealed, and   )
delivered in the presence   )
of:)
)
_____   )   _____s
for the Assignor   )   The Assignor

SELF-COUNSEL PRESS—Form 1001/04

ASSIGNMENT OF MONEY DUE

For value received, which is acknowledged, _____(the "Assignor")
(assignor name)

hereby assigns all interest and benefit in the attached statement of account (the "Account")
_____

to _____(the "Assignee").
(assignee name)

The Assignor warrants to the Assignee that:

      a) the Account is due and owing in its full face amount;

      b) no payment has been made on the Account; and

      c) there is no defence to or right of set-off or counterclaim against the Account.

Given under seal on _____.
(date)

Signed, sealed, and   )
delivered in the presence   )
of:)
)

_____)   _____s
for the Assignor   )   The Assignor

The undersigned acknowledges notice of and consents to the above assignment.

Dated_____

Witnessed by:)
)
_____)   _____s

SELF-COUNSEL PRESS—Form 1002/04

ASSIGNMENT OF REAL ESTATE CONTRACT

For value received, which is acknowledged,_____(the "Assignor")
(assignor name)

hereby assigns all interest and benefit in an agreement of purchase and sale of _____
_____

between _____ (the "Vendor")
(vendor name)

and the Assignor, accepted by the Vendor on_____
(date)

to_____(the "Assignee").
(assignee name)

The Assignor stipulates, however, that this assignment is made completely at the risk of the Assignee without any representations, warranties, or collateral assurances of any kind whatsoever with regard to the subject matter of this assignment, its ownership, or the right to make this assignment.

Given under seal on _____.
(date)

Signed, sealed, and   )
delivered in the presence   )
of:)
)
_____   )   _____s
for the Assignor   )   The Assignor

ASSIGNMENT OF CONTRACT

For value received, which is acknowledged,_____
(assignor name)

_____(the "Assignor")

hereby assigns all interest and benefit in the attached contract to_____
(assignee name)

_____(the "Assignee").

The Assignor stipulates, however, that this assignment is made completely at the risk of the Assignee without any representations, warranties, or collateral assurances of any kind whatsoever with regard to the subject matter of this assignment, its ownership or the right to make this assignment.

Given under seal on _____.
(date)

Signed, sealed, and   )
delivered in the presence   )
of:)
)
_____   )   _____s
for the Assignor   )   The Assignor

ASSIGNMENT OF COPYRIGHT

For value received, which is acknowledged,_____

(assignor name)

(the "Assignor") hereby assigns all copyright in_____

(name of work)

(the "Work") to _____(the "Assignee").

(assignee name)

The Assignor warrants to the Assignee that:

    a)   copyright exists in the Work;

    b)   the Assignor owns all the copyright in the Work;

    c)   the Assignor has the right to assign the copyright in the Work;

    d)   there is no dispute or pending dispute over the existence or ownership of copyright in the Work;

    e)   the Assignee can register and dispose of the copyright in the Work in the Assignee's own name.

Given under seal on _____.

(date)

Signed, sealed, and   )
delivered in the presence   )
of:)
)
_____   )   _____s
for the Assignor   )   The Assignor

NOTICE OF ASSIGNMENT

_____, 20__

Dear _____:

Re Notice of Assignment

This is to notify you that I have legally assigned all interest and benefit in _____

_____
(subject matter)

to _____
(name)

of _____
(address)

effective_____.
(date)

Please direct yourself to the named assignee accordingly.

Yours very truly,

_____

(Signature)

SELF-COUNSEL PRESS—Form 1006/04

CHEQUE ENDORSEMENT

a) To pay any holder of the endorsed cheque

_____
(Signature of Payee)

b) To pay a named person or according to his/her subsequent endorsement

Pay _____or Order._____
               (Name)   *(Signature of Payee)*

c) To pay only a named person (safest endorsement)

Pay _____only._____
               (Name)   *(Signature of Payee)*

11
CORPORATE

Form 1100. Notice of annual meeting of shareholders

The general bylaws of a corporation usually require proper notice to be given of a meeting of shareholders. Use this form to give formal notice of an annual meeting of shareholders.

Form 1101. Notice of special meeting of shareholders

Use this form to give formal notice of any shareholders' meeting other than the annual meeting. Attach a copy of the draft resolution as Schedule 1. This draft resolution should be self-explanatory of the nature of the special business to be transacted at the meeting.

Form 1102. Proxy form

Use this form to appoint a non-solicited proxy to attend and vote in your place at a shareholders' meeting.

Note that many jurisdictions have special rules governing solicited proxies.

Form 1103. Notice of meeting of directors

The general bylaws of a corporation usually require proper notice to be given of a meeting of directors. Use this form to give formal notice of a meeting of directors.

Form 1104. Minutes of shareholders' meeting

Minutes should be kept of every formal meeting of shareholders or directors of a corporation. Use this form as a sample for formal minutes of a meeting of shareholders to be inserted in the corporate minute book.

Form 1105. Minutes of directors' meeting

Use this form as a sample for formal minutes of a meeting of directors to be inserted in the corporate minute book. The dissenting votes, if any, should be recorded for each motion.

Form 1106 and Form 1107. Shareholders' and directors' resolutions

Many small corporations are so closely held (few shareholders and directors) that going through the motions of sending out formal notice of a meeting, holding a meeting, and keeping formal minutes of that meeting is somewhat artificial. Use Form 1106 to prepare written, unanimously signed shareholders' resolutions and Form 1107 to prepare directors' resolutions instead. Remember to store the written resolutions in the corporate minute book.

Form 1108. Bylaw

Bylaws are the internal rules governing the corporation. Use this form, with proper legal advice, to draft a corporate bylaw or amending bylaw. Note that the bylaw is passed by the directors and confirmed by the shareholders.

Form 1109. Annual directors' resolutions

Use this form, with proper legal advice, to draft annual directors' resolutions.

Form 1110. Annual shareholders' resolutions

Use this form, with proper legal advice, to draft annual shareholders' resolutions.

Form 1111. Other directors' resolutions

This form illustrates some typical written directors' resolutions.

Form 1112. Other shareholders' resolutions

This form illustrates some typical written shareholders' resolutions.

Form 1113 and Form 1114. Resignations of officer and director

Use these forms to compose a formal letter of resignation by an officer (Form 1113) or director (Form 1114) of a corporation.

Form 1115. Certificate of true copy

Use this form where a certificate of some corporate action is required.

NOTICE OF ANNUAL MEETING OF SHAREHOLDERS

_____
(corporate name)

Notice is hereby given that the Annual Meeting of shareholders of_____
(the "Corporation")

_____

will be held on_____at _____
(date)

_____
(address)

commencing at_____for the following purposes:
(time)

a)   to receive the financial statements of the Corporation for the fiscal year ended

_____.
(date)

[OPTIONAL: together with the reports of the auditors and directors on the statements, and to appoint auditors for the current fiscal year of the Corporation];

b)   to elect directors for the Corporation;

c)   to transact any other business that may properly come before the meeting and any adjournments.

Dated at_____on _____.
(place)   (date)

By Order of the Board of Directors

_____
(Signature of secretary)

_____
(Secretary name, typed)

Corporate Secretary

NOTICE OF SPECIAL MEETING OF SHAREHOLDERS

_____

(corporate name)

Notice is hereby given that a Special Meeting of shareholders of_____

(the "Corporation")

will be held on_____at_____

(date)   *(address)*

_____

commencing at_____for the following purposes:

(time)

    a)   to consider passage of the resolution appended to this notice as Schedule 1;

    b)   to transact any other business that may properly come before the meeting and any adjournments.

Dated at_____on_____.

(place)   *(date)*

By Order of the Board of Directors

_____

(Signature of secretary)

_____

(Secretary name, typed)

Corporate Secretary

PROXY FORM

_____
(corporate name)

The undersigned shareholder of_____
(corporate name)

hereby appoints_____
(proxy name)

as the nominee of the undersigned to attend and act for the undersigned at the meeting of shareholders of the corporation to be held on_____
(date)

at_____
(address)

and at any adjournments of that meeting in the same manner and with the same power, including with respect to voting, as the undersigned if the undersigned were present in person.

Dated_____
(date)

_____
(Signature of witness)

Witness

_____
(Signature of shareholder)

_____
(Shareholder name, typed)

NOTICE OF MEETING OF DIRECTORS

_____
(corporate name)

Notice is hereby given that a meeting of the Board of Directors of

_____
(corporate name)

will be held on_____at_____
(date)

_____
(address)

commencing at_____.
(time)

Dated at_____on_____.
(place)   (date)

By Order of the Board of Directors

_____
(Signature of secretary)

_____
(Secretary name, typed)

Corporate Secretary

SELF-COUNSEL PRESS – FORM 1103/05

MINUTES OF SHAREHOLDERS' MEETING

_____
(corporate name)

A meeting of shareholders of_____
(corporate name)

was duly called and held on_____at _____
(date)

_____
(address)

commencing at_____.
(time)

With the approval of the shareholders present, _____
(chair name)

acted as Chair of the meeting and_____
(secretary name)

recorded the minutes.

The Chair noted that the required quorum of shareholders was present to conduct business and that the meeting was properly constituted.

On motions duly made and seconded, it was voted that:

1. The minutes of the last meeting of shareholders be taken as read.

2. _(insert resolution per numbered paragraph)_

There being no further business to transact at this time, it was voted to adjourn the meeting.

Dated_____
(date)

_____   _____
(Signature of secretary)   (Signature of chair)

_____   _____
(Secretary name, typed)   (Chair name, typed)

Secretary   Chair

MINUTES OF DIRECTORS' MEETING

_____
(corporate name)

Minutes of a meeting of the Board of Directors of_____
(corporate name)

duly called and held on_____at_____
(date)

_____
(address)

commencing at_____.
(time)

Present were:

With the approval of the directors present, _____
(chair name)

acted as Chair of the meeting and_____
(secretary name)

recorded the minutes.

On motions duly made and seconded, it was voted that:

1. The minutes of the last meeting of directors be taken as read.

2. _(insert resolution per numbered paragraph)_

Dissenting to the motion were

_____

_____

_____
(dissenting names)

There being no further business to transact at this time, it was voted to adjourn the meeting.

Dated_____
(date)

_____   _____
(Signature of secretary)   _(Signature of chair)_

_____   _____
(Secretary name, typed)   _(Chair name, typed)_

Secretary   Chair

SELF-COUNSEL PRESS – FORM 1105/05

SHAREHOLDERS' RESOLUTIONS

The undersigned, being all the voting shareholders of

_____
(corporate name)

hereby sign the following resolutions:

RESOLVED THAT

    1.   *(insert resolution per numbered paragraph)*

Dated_____
(date)

_____   _____
(Signature of shareholder)   *(Signature of shareholder)*

_____   _____
(Shareholder name, typed)   *(Shareholder name, typed)*

DIRECTORS' RESOLUTIONS

The undersigned, being all the directors of

_____
(corporate name)

hereby sign the following resolutions:

RESOLVED THAT

    1. (insert resolution per numbered paragraph)

Dated_____
             (date)

_____   _____
(Signature of director)   *(Signature of director)*

_____   _____
(Director name, typed)   *(Director name, typed)*

BYLAW

_____
(corporate name)

Bylaw No._____
      (number)

A bylaw to_____

Be it enacted as Bylaw No._____
                         (number)

of_____
        (corporate name)

(the "Corporation") that:

The directors and officers of the Corporation are instructed and authorized to take such action and execute such instruments as are required or deemed advisable to implement this bylaw.

Passed by the undersigned, being all the directors of_____
                                                            (corporate name)

on_____
        (date)

_____   _____
(Signature of director)   *(Signature of director)*

_____   _____
(Director name, typed)   *(Director name, typed)*

Confirmed by the undersigned, being all the shareholders of_____,
                                                                  (corporate name)

on_____
        (date)

_____   _____
(Signature of shareholder)   *(Signature of shareholder*

_____   _____
(Shareholder name, typed)   *(Shareholder name, typed)*

ANNUAL DIRECTORS' RESOLUTIONS

The undersigned, being all the directors of _____
(corporate name)

hereby sign the following resolutions:

RESOLVED THAT

1. The financial statements of the corporation for the fiscal year ended _____
    (date)

    prepared by_____ chartered accountants, under their
    (accountants)

    comments dated _____ are approved, which approval shall be evidenced
    (date)

    by signature of the balance sheet.

[OR]

1. The financial statements of the corporation for the fiscal year ended _____
    (date)

    prepared by_____ under their audit report dated
    (auditors)

    _____ are approved, which approval shall be evidenced by signature of
    (date)

    the balance sheet.

2. The approved financial statements be placed before the annual meeting of shareholders of
    the corporation.

3. _____ are appointed the accountants of the corporation for the
    (accountants)

    current fiscal year.

Dated _____
(date)

_____   _____
(Signature of director)   (Signature of director)

_____   _____
(Director name, typed)   (Director name, typed)

SELF-COUNSEL PRESS – FORM 1109/05

ANNUAL SHAREHOLDERS' RESOLUTIONS

The undersigned, being all the shareholders of _____
(corporate name)

hereby sign the following annual resolutions:

RESOLVED THAT

1. These resolutions are in place of an annual meeting of shareholders of the corporation.

2. The financial statements of the corporation for the fiscal year ended _____
    (date)

    prepared by_____ Chartered accountants, under their comments dated

    _____ are received.
    (date)

    [OR]

2. The financial statements of the corporation for the fiscal year ended _____
    (date)

    prepared by_____ under their audit report dated_____
    (auditors)   *(date)*

    are approved.

3. _____ and _____ are continued as
    (director's name)   *(director's name)*

    directors of the corporation.

4. No auditor be appointed for the current fiscal year of the corporation.

    [OR]

4. _____ are appointed the auditors of the corporation for the
    (auditors)

    current fiscal year.

5. The acts of the Board of Directors since the last annual meeting of the shareholders are approved and ratified.

Dated _____
      (date)

_____
(Signature of shareholder)

_____
(Signature of shareholder)

_____
(Shareholder name, typed)

_____
(Shareholder name, typed)

SELF-COUNSEL PRESS – FORM 1110/05

OTHER DIRECTORS' RESOLUTIONS

RESOLVED THAT

1. Bylaw No._____ is passed as a bylaw of the corporation to be placed before a meeting of shareholders of the corporation for confirmation.

2. The application to amend the Articles of Incorporation [OR Letters Patent] of the corporation in the draft form appended as Schedule A to these resolutions is approved to be placed before a meeting of shareholders of the corporation for confirmation.

3. The corporation sell substantially all its assets to_____
(name)

   in accordance with the draft agreement of purchase and sale appended as Schedule A to these resolutions.

4. _____is elected as Chair of the Board of Directors.
(chair name)

5. A dividend of $_____ per share is declared on the issued

   _____shares of the corporation held by the
(class name)

   _____shareholders of record as of this date.
(class name)

6. The salary of the _____of the corporation is fixed at
(officer)

   $_____per annum effective _____
(date)

7. The corporation execute the _____in the draft
(contract/instrument)

   form appended as Schedule A to these resolutions.

8. The transfer of_____from_____to
(number and class of shares)   (name)

   _____is approved.
(name)

9. The address of the head/registered office of the corporation is changed to

   _____.
(address)

OTHER SHAREHOLDERS' RESOLUTIONS

RESOLVED THAT

1. _____ is elected as a director of the corporation.
    (director name)

2. Bylaw No._____passed by the Board of Directors of the corporation is confirmed.

3. The application to amend the Articles of Incorporation [OR Letters Patent] of the corporation in the draft form appended as Schedule A to these resolutions is approved.

4. The proposed sale by the corporation of substantially all its assets to_____
    _____in accordance with the draft agreement of
    (purchaser name)
    purchase and sale appended as Schedule B to these resolutions is approved.

5. _____is removed as a director of the corporation.
    (director name)

RESIGNATION OF OFFICER

To:_____
(corporate name)

Re Resignation of Office

I hereby resign as a director of_____
(office)

_____
(corporate name)

effective immediately.

Dated_____
(date)

Yours very truly,

_____

(Signature of resigning officer)

_____

(Resigning officer name, typed)

RESIGNATION OF DIRECTOR

To:_____

(corporate name)

Re Resignation of Directorship

I hereby resign as a director of_____

(corporate name)

effective immediately.

Dated_____

(date)

Yours very truly,

_____

(Signature of director)

_____

(Director name, typed)

CERTIFICATE OF TRUE COPY

_____
(corporate name)

CERTIFICATE

The undersigned Secretary of_____
(corporate name)

hereby certifies that Schedule A appended to this certificate is a true copy of a_____

_____
(describe instrument)

passed by the shareholders [OR directors] of the corporation on_____.
(date)

Certified by me under the corporate seal of the corporation on_____.
(date)

_____c/s
(Signature of secretary)

_____
(Secretary name, typed)

Secretary

12
MISCELLANEOUS

Form 1200. Unilateral release of liability

Use this form to draft a unilateral (from one side) release of liability in connection with the final settlement of a potential claim against the other side.

Insert description of potential liability situation at end of first paragraph.

Form 1201. Mutual release of liability

Use this form to draft a mutual (by both sides) release of liabilities in connection with final settlement of mutual potential claims.

Insert description of potential mutual liability situation at end of first paragraph.

Form 1202. Trade secret non-disclosure agreement

Use this form, with proper legal advice, to exact a non-disclosure of trade secrets covenant from an associated independent business.

Form 1203. Declaration of trust

Occasionally, someone might want to hold property in other than his or her own name. The person in whose name the property is held usually holds it in secret trust but this can create problems of proof (e.g., where a secret trustee dies apparently owning the property) if there is nothing in writing. Use this form, with proper legal advice on the implications and effectiveness of using the device, to document a secret trust.

UNILATERAL RELEASE OF LIABILITY

In consideration of the payment of_____dollars ($ _____),

receipt of which is acknowledged, _____(the "Claimant")
(claimant name)

hereby finally and irrevocably releases_____ (the "Payer")
(payer name)

from all liability to the Claimant, and settles all actions or causes of action against the Payer, for damages, loss or injury sustained by the Claimant, however arising, present and future, known and unknown at this time, relating to:

If the Claimant has instituted any legal proceedings against the Payer settled by this release, the Claimant covenants to have them dismissed at the Claimant's cost with express prejudice to bringing further proceedings against the Payer arising out of the same matter.

The Claimant also covenants not to make any claim or institute any proceedings against any person who might claim over against or claim contribution or indemnity from the Payer in connection with any matter for which this release is given.

The Claimant also acknowledges that the Payer does not admit liability to the Claimant in connection with any matter for which this release is given.

Given under seal on _____.
(date)

Signed, sealed, and   )
delivered in the presence   )
of:)
)
_____   )   _____s
for the Claimant   )   *(Claimant signature)*

SELF-COUNSEL PRESS—Form 1200/04

MUTUAL RELEASE OF LIABILITY

The undersigned hereby finally and irrevocably mutually release each other from all liability to each other and settle all actions and causes of action against each other for damages, loss, or injury sustained by either of them, however arising, present and future, known and unknown at this time, relating to:

If either party has instituted any legal proceedings against the other settled by this release, that party covenants to have them dismissed at that party's cost with express prejudice to bringing further proceedings against the other arising out of the same matter.

It is agreed that neither party to this mutual release will make any claim or take any proceedings against any person who might claim over against or claim contribution or indemnity from the other party in connection with any matter for which this mutual release is given.

It is understood and agreed that nothing in this mutual release is to be construed as an admission of liability in connection with any matter for which this mutual release is given.

Executed in duplicate under seal on _____.
                                                                 (date)

Signed, sealed, and   )
delivered in the presence   )
of:)
)
_____   )
)   _____ s
)   *(Party One signature)*
)
_____   )
)   _____ s
)   *(Party Two signature)*

TRADE SECRET NON-DISCLOSURE AGREEMENT

Whereas _____ (the "Confider")
(confider name)

is prepared to disclose certain trade secrets relating to_____

_____ (the "trade secrets")
(insert details)

to _____ (the "Confidant")
(confidant name)

for mutual business purposes;

The Confidant hereby covenants:

a) to protect the confidentiality of the trade secrets and not to disclose them to any third-party;

b) to exploit the trade secrets only for the Confider's and the Confidant's mutual business purposes and not to exploit them for the Confidant's sole business purposes.

The Confidant accepts that, if any part of these covenants is void or unenforceable for any reason, it shall be severed without affecting the validity of the balance of the covenants.

Given under seal on _____.
(date)

Signed, sealed, and   )
delivered in the presence   )
of:)
)
_____   )   _____s
for the Confidant   )   The Confidant

SELF-COUNSEL PRESS—Form 1202/04

DECLARATION OF TRUST

This declaration of trust is made by (1)_____ (the "Trustee")

(trustee name)

in favour of (2) _____(the "Beneficiary").

(beneficiary name)

The Trustee solemnly declares that he holds _____

(list details)

_____(the "Property")

in trust solely for the benefit of the Beneficiary.

The Trustee further promises the Beneficiary:

a) not to deal with the Property in any way, except to transfer it to the Beneficiary, without the instructions and consent of the Beneficiary; and

b) to account to the Beneficiary for any money received by the Trustee, other than from Beneficiary, in connection with holding the Property.

Given under seal on _____.

(date)

Signed, sealed, and)
delivered in the presence)
of:)
)
_____)   _____s
) *(Trustee signature)*

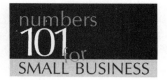

Numbers 101 for Small Business is a series of easy-to-understand guides for small-business owners, covering such topics as bookkeeping, analyzing and tracking financial information, starting a business, and growing a business. Using real-life examples, Angie Mohr teaches small-business owners how to beat the odds and turn their ideas into successful, growing companies. Mohr is a chartered accountant and certified management accountant.

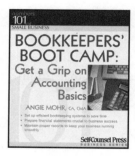

Bookkeepers' Boot Camp: Get a Grip on Accounting Basics

ISBN 10: 1-55180-449-2
ISBN 13: 978-1-55180-449-1
$14.95 US / $19.95 CDN

Bookkeepers' Boot Camp teaches you how to sort through the masses of information and paperwork, how to record what is important for your business, and how to grow your business for success!

- Understand the balance sheet
- Learn the basics of income statements and cash-flow statements
- Record the sales cycle
- Learn how to account for inventory
- Monitor your budget and cash flow

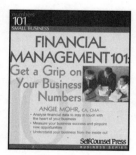

Financial Management 101: Get a Grip on Your Business Numbers

ISBN 10: 1-55180-448-4
ISBN 13: 978-1-55180-448-4
$14.95 US / $19.95 CDN

Financial Management 101 addresses business planning, from understanding financial statements to budgeting for advertising. Angie Mohr's easy-to-understand approach to small-business planning and management ensures that the money coming in is always greater than the money going out!

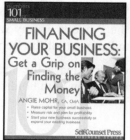

Financing Your Business: Get a Grip on Finding the Money

ISBN 10: 1-55180-583-9
ISBN 13: 978-1-55180-583-2
$14.95 US / $19.95 CDN

Financing Your Business will show you, in an easy-to-understand manner, how to raise capital for your small business. Whether you are just starting a new business or you want to expand an existing business, this book leads you step by step through the process and explores all the options available so that you can devise a financial plan that is suited to your company and goals.

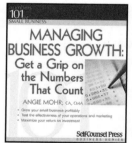

Managing Business Growth: Get a Grip on the Numbers That Count

ISBN 10: 1-55180-581-2
ISBN 13: 978-1-55180-581-8
$14.95 US / $19.95 CDN

In *Managing Business Growth,* Angie Mohr teaches small-business owners how to profitably expand their businesses by using sound financial planning. This book shows you how to measure the effectiveness of your operations, manage human resources, pinpoint new opportunities, and maximize profits.